Hunting. . .
What Youth
Need to Know

D1622612

By Craig Boddington

Published by
the Conklin Endowment Fund

Table of Contents

Foreword

Perhaps the most misunderstood sporting activity is hunting—not curling, nor La Crosse. My grandson plays La Crosse, and I discovered it is the only native North American sport. I watched a few of his games and quickly understood the rules and format. Unfortunately, hunting is not that easy to fully understand in today's environment.

Man has hunted for thousands of years. He had to hunt to exist. So it should be simple, man hunts today for existence, but also for sport, which confuses many non-hunters. These are the same non-hunters who eat meat and enjoy a spectrum of animal by-products.

The anti-hunter program only came into prominence sometime after the end of the Viet Nam War. Maybe the anti-war city youth of the time carried their despise for war to people with guns who hunted. Maybe they tried hard, very hard, to convince their children of their views. There is no proof of this, but circumstantially the times and events from large metropolitan cities almost merge.

The purpose of this book is to explain the complexities, to provide facts, and to do this in a text both young people, especially, and adults, especially teachers, can understand. After all, there are always two sides to every debate, and a wise person, and most smart young people, will want to know both sides of the question to make their own unbiased decision.

Young people I know, including my own nine grandchildren, want to make their own decisions. This book provides that fair opportunity.

Craig Boddington is one of the most experienced of any person in the country to explain the hunters' platform. He is a renowned writer of many books and hundreds of magazine articles, television activist, hunter, husband,

and father. He realizes we are at a time in history when a hunting platform has to be explained. Most non-hunters do not know, for example, that large and thriving herds of wildlife in all 50 states in this country are only due to conservation efforts of all hunters through hunting license dues and through conservation efforts of many kinds for wildlife by the organizations, hunting clubs, and individuals who hunt and who can afford it.

I learned by reading this book and I have hunted for a long time. The author is very thorough. Hunting and guns are important topics for young people to be familiar with, and this book provides, in easy terms, a wealth of knowledge for one side of the debate.

I challenge young people to read this book. How can you not want to understand the hunters' side of an activity that millions of people in the United States, people in every state, enjoy? Hunters have been too quiet, not vocal, and too assuming. Learn about them.

I challenge non-hunters to read this book. Most non-hunters pretend to know about hunting, but I do not believe they do. I believe they know what somebody has told them, and they have not done enough individual research so their opinions end up biased. Most are surprised by what they learn.

Tom Hammond
President
The Conklin Foundation

✢ CHAPTER ONE ✢

The Hunter's Horn

This book is presented by the directors of the Conklin Foundation and the Conklin Endowment Fund. The organization is named after the late Dr. Jim Conklin, a successful surgeon by vocation and a serious hunter by avocation. "Dr. Jim," as we called him, believed in ethical hunting and loved the most challenging hunting situations; he also understood not only the importance of hunting to conservation but also how important it is to pass on the traditions of both hunting and conservation to future generations. We who maintain the foundation in his memory are thus hunters. We make no apologies, nor do we believe apologies are necessary.

Humans have evolved as hunting animals, for better or worse the most successful predator this planet has yet witnessed. Predator? Yes, we humans have eyes that look forward, a characteristic shared with other predators, such as felines, canines, and bears. It is true that we are omnivorous rather than carnivorous and, over the eons, a more balanced diet has undoubtedly contributed to our much greater longevity, allowing us more time on Earth to use what evolved as our greatest weapon and tool for survival, the human brain.

Compared to the great cats and the big bears, humans are actually very puny creatures. Our opposing thumbs, coupled with our developing brains, enabled us to make and use tools. Some of those tools were used to defeat— prey upon, successfully hunt, defend ourselves against—animals more powerful than ourselves. Some anthropologists theorize that the high protein diet of the earliest humanoid hunters enabled more rapid development of our large and complex brains but that certainly we developed as hunters and hunter–gatherers, never as browsers or grazers.

Even today, in the twenty-first century, small groups of humans remain—tribes—who still function effectively as hunter–gatherers. Some augment their traditional equipment with modern tools and weapons. A classic example might be the Inuits of Canada's Nunavut. However, in the remote corners of the world a few societies still exist that continue existences that we consider Stone Age, Bronze Age, or early Iron Age. Some continue by choice, ignoring our modern world, and others by isolation. We of the modern world consider them curiosities, only rarely pondering how they might consider us. But whether we're talking about the San, better known as the Bushmen of the Kalahari; the pygmies of the African forests; the head-hunting tribes of New Guinea; or the Indians of the Amazon Basin, peoples remain who live according to their traditions, and although the wildlife and methods vary, they are universally hunters.

In our modern society, not all of us are hunters. This is probably a good thing. We have become the world's most numerous large mammal, and neither the habitat nor the wildlife resources remain for all of us to live as hunter–gatherers. Those of us who are active hunters have dwindled in many parts of the world. This is largely a reflection of the urbanization of society. Numbers of people making their living from agriculture have also dwindled, certainly in the Western world. Here in the United States the number of hunters is generally quoted at about sixteen million. According to the National Shooting Sports Foundation and the U.S. Fish and Wildlife's most recent survey, there has actually been an increase in hunting license sales during the past few years (2008–2012), but the actual number of active hunters is almost impossible to track. Many people, especially those who make their living on the land, traditionally purchase hunting licenses in support of their local wildlife, but not all of them actively participate in hunting. And there are many people who don't buy hunting licenses every year but who certainly consider themselves hunters. The numbers are also skewed by the fact that many states offer lifetime hunting licenses and many jurisdictions don't require licenses for hunters above a certain age. As our society grows older and older people remain more active, this can be a very significant number.

Whatever the actual number, the United States holds by far the world's largest group of hunters. To some degree this is a reflection of our North American model of wildlife management, which places wildlife in the public stewardship, allowing access to much of our vast holdings of public land and depending heavily upon hunting and fishing license fees to fund management costs. Our North American model is quite unique in the world and will be discussed in greater detail in later chapters. For now, let's just say that American hunters are a very large and active group; few societies in the world can claim active, participating hunters in the *millions*. That said, even if the number of us American hunters is increasing, we are decreasing as a percentage of the population.

For many people, perhaps especially our tens of millions of urban dwellers, the entire concept of hunting is totally unfamiliar. This creates a significant challenge for both sides: those of us totally immersed in the activity and its lifestyle and those to whom hunting is a foreign concept. Hunters find it difficult to explain why they hunt to people with no knowledge or understanding of the activity. For most of us the answer is simple: It's an integral part of who and what we are, part of our innate genetic programming, an activity that inspires the deepest passions in those of us who pursue it, which is even harder to explain to people who have no interest or exposure and little knowledge of hunting.

It is perhaps most traditional for the passion for the outdoors to be passed along from father to son and, today, from parent to child, but this simply means exposure and opportunity. Many people who might have that spark hidden in their genes never have the opportunity for it to burst into flame, and many, regardless of opportunity, simply don't have it. This concept is hard to explain, but the evidence is there. Often hunters are encountered who, lacking the early advantage of a hunting family, came to hunting later in life. Most were introduced by friends who were hunters, but one occasionally encounters a hardy and courageous soul who, inevitably driven to hunting, found his or her own way, which, as you can imagine, is no easier than starting into any other complex undertaking with no background or formal training. These late-blooming hunters are no less avid than those introduced at a young age and very possibly savor the experience even more, recognizing the lost time.

The late Robert Chester Ruark, widely syndicated columnist, best-selling novelist, lifelong bird hunter, and in the last fifteen years of his short life (1915–1965) an avid big-game hunter, captured this thought as well as anyone ever has. In context, the following quote was penned early in his superb 1953 book *Horn of the Hunter*, a nonfiction account of his first safari to Tanganyika, a book that still captures and encapsulates not only the magic of Africa but also the magic of hunting as well as anyone ever has:

> The hunter's horn sounds early for some, later for others. For some unfortunates, poisoned by city sidewalks and sentenced to a cement jungle more horrifying than anything to be found in Tanganyika, the horn of the hunter never winds at all. But deep in the guts of most men is buried the involuntary response to the hunter's horn, a prickle of the nape hairs, an acceleration of the pulse, an atavistic memory of his fathers, who killed first with stone, and then with club, and then with spear, and then with bow, and then with gun, and finally with formulae. How meek the man is of no importance; somewhere in the pigeon chest of the clerk is still the vestigial remnant of the hunter's heart; somewhere in his nostrils the half-forgotten smell of blood.

Ruark alludes to the converse: Regardless of exposure, opportunity, coaching, and coaxing, hunting is not for everyone. It is a dream of most parents for their children to follow in their footsteps, at least in the good things in their lives. Many hunters are thus disappointed that their children have little or no interest in hunting, but this is sometimes the case. In our experience there is little to be done about this, so it is probably as it should be: The hunter's horn doesn't sound for everyone.

Many hunters have seen this in their own families, where, despite equal opportunity and exposure, one child becomes a lifelong hunter, whereas a sibling has little interest. Here we must take exception with Mr. Ruark for his consistent use of male pronouns. He can be forgiven because, traditionally and still so in the 1950s, hunting was primarily a male pastime. Mind you, there have always been notable and accomplished female hunters, but we men have strived for eons to keep the hunting to ourselves and leave the gathering to the distaff side. So, historically and traditionally, far fewer women than men have been introduced to hunting. This is changing—and for the better. The primary growth in both shooting sports and hunting has been among females, and it is becoming clear that the hunter's horn sounds equally to both sexes—some men won't hear it, and some women will.

Founded by Theodore Roosevelt and some of his friends back in 1887, the Boone and Crockett Club is America's oldest hunting and conservation organization. One of its activities is maintaining records of North American big game, with the size of horns, antlers, and skulls (in bears and cats) measured in accordance with their criteria. Every three years, called an awards period, the club convenes its members and recognizes the largest North American animals taken within that period. Their twenty-eighth awards presentation was held in July 2013, with special and separate recognition given to young hunters and adults who took exceptional trophies. Among the adults, women were a relatively small percentage, but among the young hunters, under the age of 18 when their big animals were taken, the award recipients were forty percent female. Truly the guard is changing!

This volume is not specifically intended for hunters, which, as we've seen, are a relatively small minority of the population. It is also not intended for the equally small (possibly smaller) minority of decided anti-hunters. They are zealots, as hunters are zealots, and it is extremely difficult, if not almost impossible, to change the minds of people truly committed to any cause, course of action, or set of beliefs. There is little point in boring them with facts. This book is intended primarily for the great majority of people who are undecided and uncommitted regarding the question of hunting. It is especially intended for young people, who are often bombarded with slanted rhetoric from outspoken anti-hunting and anti-firearms individuals but who should be equally presented with facts from the other side and thus be able to make up their own minds.

The reality is that most people in our modern world have no exposure to hunting, and it has little or no visible impact on their lives. However, regarding almost any activity that has no direct effect on us, most people take a let-do attitude. For instance, people who are terrified of heights probably don't pursue rock climbing or skydiving but have no problem with climbers and parachutists, and they will defend their right to pursue their hobbies that, after all, have no impact on society and create risk only to themselves. Similarly, sports men and women don't expect the vast majority of uncommitted non-hunters to become fascinated by their sport. However, we ask them—many of *you*—to keep an open mind. Unlike mountain climbing and skydiving, which certainly are heroic and admirable activities, carefully regulated sport hunting does carry benefits for everyone in the conservation, preservation, and management of wildlife.

In chapters to come we will discuss the development of wildlife management as it exists today and the role played by regulated sport hunting. If our goal is achieved, then new members of that great non-hunting majority will be armed with facts and examples that will allow them to reach their own decisions. And some may feel that innate spark and pledge themselves to giving it a try, to see for themselves what this part of the outdoor world is all about.

It should be said here that, in the United States and in most modern societies, hunting is *not* a right. In accordance with the Second Amendment to our Constitution, our ability to keep and bear arms *is* a right, and the importance of that right will be discussed. But using those arms to hunt is a privilege that must be conducted in accordance with local, state, and federal laws. Our North American system of hunting laws was created by hunters in a time when a much larger percentage of the population hunted, primarily for subsistence. They were created to ensure that wildlife would persist for future generations to enjoy and, as required, utilize. The success of these efforts can be seen in each and every one of our fifty states and in all the provinces of Canada. Hunters as a group and generally today on a global basis are among the most self-limiting people on Earth, continually creating and, in the vast majority, adhering to additional rules that limit and regulate their activities for the benefit of the resource and future generations.

We simply ask that our non-hunting readers keep an open mind and consider the facts that we will put forth in this volume. This is not necessarily an easy assignment because hunting stirs human emotions at both ends of the scale, for hunters and anti-hunters alike. Our goal, which is also not a simple task, is to avoid our own emotions as passionate hunters and lay out, pragmatically, practically, and we hope reasonably, the essential role hunting plays in modern wildlife management and conservation, allowing wildlife to persist, exist, and in many cases flourish so that all—hunters, non-hunters, and anti-hunters alike—may enjoy and admire wild animals in a world that, increasingly, is no longer wild. If that goal is achieved, then perhaps more of the neutral majority will defend the committed minority's privilege to pursue their passion. Desiring to participate is not required, nor is it a goal; as hunters we ask only that our essential role in conserving, protecting, and propagating wildlife be acknowledged.

However, it is not impossible that some currently neutral readers will someday hear the hunter's horn. Try it; you might like it. Most people, men and women of all ages, enjoy the outdoor experience of which hunting is just one part. A great many people, if exposed to ethical sport hunting, will feel "the involuntary response to the hunter's horn, a prickle of the nape hairs, an acceleration of the pulse." But some will not. To those who read this book who are already hunters, a caution should be offered: Once again, as a foot-stomping point, hunting isn't for everyone. If it's in your genes, then it's there. If it isn't, one may go through the motions as a social exercise or familial duty. The experience will probably be enjoyable rather than distasteful, but the passion is unlikely to be kindled.

For family members or curious non-hunting friends, the best hunters can do is offer exposure and opportunity and see whether it takes. It is not an activity that can or should be forced. Many of us who are hunters have observed our friends pushing children or spouses toward the activity when, from the outside looking in, it has seemed obvious that there was little or no genuine enthusiasm. Generally speaking the passion is either there, hidden within, or it isn't. However, while it's a simple fact that the hunter's horn sounds equally for both men and women—and for some of each sex, not at all—it's also a fact that the hunter's horn might be heard earlier for some and later for others.

In the United States it has long been a tradition that, as part of our complex system of hunting laws, minimum ages are established to obtain a hunting license. This varies considerably; some states establish twelve as a minimum age, whereas others allow small-game and bird hunting for younger hunters but require a person to be fourteen to hunt larger game. These laws are changing and in many cases being done away with; it is more widely accepted today that some young people are ready at earlier ages than others and that only a parent or adult mentor is in a position to make that judgment. Some young people have demonstrated their capability to be safe and competent in the field at the age of eight or even younger and many more at the more traditional age of eleven or twelve. Still others don't hear the horn until their midteens, and, as mentioned, usually because of a lack of previous exposure or opportunity, new hunters take to the field in all stages of adulthood.

The converse is also true. There are many people who hunted with their families as youngsters but as adults, perhaps because of occupations or geographic locations, no longer participate because of lack of opportunity. Some return to it later in life, when time becomes more available; others remain part of that non-hunting majority. But there is one common thread: Very few people who have been exposed to lawful, ethical hunting ever join that small minority of committed anti-hunters. The tones of the hunter's horn may grow soft and almost silent for some, but it's always there, somewhere in the background.

Chapter Two

The Tradition Continues

Hunting for food remains critical to many people in rural areas throughout the world. Even here in the United States subsistence hunting is an important motivation for being in the field if not for sheer survival, then to augment a meager table. However, in modern Western civilization hunting is rarely a matter of life and death. And yet, in the United States, hunting remains an important activity for, literally, millions of people. For some it's a social event, a chance to spend quality time in camp and in the woods with friends and family members. For others it's a statement: putting unadulterated meat on the table that wasn't wrapped in cellophane.

To many of us hunters it's a lifestyle issue: Hunting is part of who we are and, seasonally, what we do. With some important spring exceptions, such as wild turkeys and, in some jurisdictions, the spring bear season, hunting in North America is primarily an autumn and winter activity. Seasons and bag limits vary depending on equipment used and management goals, but hunting seasons are finite, as decreed by hunters for hunters (and for wildlife) generations ago. And yet recent surveys have shown that as many as ten million Americans identify themselves as deer hunters. This does not mean that they just hunt deer during the season, although that is certainly implied. Rather, this is a statement they use to define themselves and their most preferred pastime, even though the actual period of time they are able to hunt deer is, in most states, limited to just a few weeks.

This is clearly an interesting sociological comment, and from the standpoint of modern hunting it bears further discussion. As this book progresses we will talk a bit about international hunting and "trophy hunting," which I put in quotes because this seems to be an aspect of hunting that both antihunters and non-hunters have the most problem with. Few people challenge pure subsistence hunting, and most people seem accepting of legal, ethical hunting as an outdoor pastime, provided the meat is utilized. It's not clear how this happened, but somewhere along the way some folks who were either misguided or very devious managed to separate in uninformed people's minds the search for larger, older animals from the utilization of meat.

This is not the way it works. In the vast majority of all sport-hunting situations wild meat harvested is fully utilized. In most North American jurisdictions recovery of meat harvested is a matter of law: Hunters are required to recover edible game meat, but one of several unique principles of our North American system of wildlife management—we call it the North American model—is that game meat cannot be sold. It is generally utilized by the people who harvest it and is shared with family and friends, but surplus game meat is often donated, with organized drives, such as Safari Club International's Hunters for the Hungry, common throughout America. Elsewhere in the world game meat is also fully utilized, but the rules are different. In other Western societies game meat has high value and is often sold in markets or directly to restaurants; in most Third World situations, such as in Africa, game meat is usually distributed to local villages. But for any ethical sport hunter, utilization of meat is absolutely mandatory.

Yes, there are exceptions. Predators are often considered unfit for human consumption. For this very reason, a fair number of serious and dedicated hunters do not hunt cats, bears, and canines. The opposite position, often defended against hunters who disagree, is that man has altered the balance literally throughout the world. Since we have done this and cannot undo it, we have become the stewards of the wild world. As good and hopefully wise stewards we must manage both prey species and predators. We will discuss these issues in later chapters and also the purely pragmatic approach that seems essential in the Third World: Large predators are destructive of livestock and often hazardous to humans. They are thus a dangerous nuisance that will be tolerated only if they have value.

For now, let's stick with the culture of hunting. The international hunting community, of which we of the Conklin Foundation are certainly members, is actually quite small, somewhere into the tens of thousands in the United States and perhaps a few hundred thousand worldwide. In reality, according to the National Shooting Sports Foundation surveys, most American hunters rarely leave their home states to hunt. This means that most hunters spend the majority of their time afield pursuing game that is available and accessible relatively close to their homes. This most available and thus most popular game has changed over time, depending on where you are.

According to some estimates there might have been ten million white-tailed deer in North America when the Pilgrims landed. Much of the East was heavily forested, and unbroken forest is not ideal habitat for white-tailed deer—but there were lots of deer, and they served as a staple food source that was hunted with little regulation until, by 1900, only some five hundred thousand remained. Don't fear for the whitetail deer; today they have not just recovered but have swollen their ranks to perhaps thirty-six million! But the point is that, by 1900, our remaining deer were pushed into the most remote and inaccessible mountains, swamps, and forests.

Some deer always remained in the Adirondacks and Appalachians and in the southern swamps and northern forests, but in the more vulnerable, open spaces of the Great Plains, deer were almost extinct. So, just a century ago, with so little opportunity across much of the country, American hunters were not deer hunters. And yet many Americans were still hunters. Many hunted small game, and waterfowl hunting was popular. But even into the 1930s market hunting was still practiced. That took its toll, as did the long drought we now call the Dust Bowl. A majority of the many reservoirs and impoundments that now dot the United States didn't yet exist, and by the 1930s our waterfowl were also in trouble.

But at the same time, farming practices supported high numbers of up-land birds: grouse in New England and the Upper Midwest and bobwhite quail in the South and Midwest. And the introduced ring-necked pheasant was on the march in the northern Great Plains. So in the 1940s avid hunters were most likely to be upland bird hunters. This situation existed through the 1950s and on into the 1960s, but things would change again. By the 1970s farming practices had changed to cleaner, more extensive farming, with less milo and more corn. Grouse and quail populations were notably in decline, undoubtedly from a variety of factors. But with protection waterfowl had rebounded, and new reservoirs held unprecedented numbers of ducks and geese. Grouse and quail hunters became waterfowl hunters, and soon they would become deer hunters. From the 1940s forward whitetail populations gradually increased, and then, in different areas at different times, the whitetail populations exploded and their growth became exponential. Seasons had to be lengthened and bag limits increased to control the number of deer, and areas closed to deer hunting for generations had to reopen hunting as an essential management tool. Iowa was the second to last U.S. state to open a modern deer season; Kansas was the last. Deer were declared extinct in Kansas—totally gone—in 1925. In 1964 Kansas reopened deer hunting. Since then both the herd and harvest goals have continued to increase, with Kansas now making available close to one hundred eighty thousand deer permits.

Yes, just like across so much of the country, the majority of modern Kansas hunters consider themselves deer hunters. But despite their favorite outdoor pastime, most hunters pursue a variety of game, so long as it's close to their homes. So there are rabbit hunters, squirrel hunters, and woodchuck hunters, and there are still waterfowl hunters and upland game hunters, and 'possum and raccoon hunters who run their hounds through snake-infested swamps all night long. And, thanks to another awesome recovery, there are probably more turkey hunters than, excepting deer hunters, all of these put together! In 1900 the wild turkey was nearly gone. Today they number in the millions and have created their own hunting cult, including a related industry of calls, camouflage, decoys, and other paraphernalia.

Name a game animal, and you will find a few die-hard purists who live to pursue only that creature. Most hunters, however, follow the seasons, pursuing some variety of game that can be had in reasonable proximity to their homes and thus available without stretching the family budget (and putting food on the table as a bonus). This is America, and these are hunters. Some dream of hunting creatures beyond the far horizons, and some cross those horizons, but, statistically, eighty percent of America's sixteen million hunters never hunt outside of their home states. Statistically, also, regardless of what other game they might hunt as the seasons allow, more than sixty percent of American hunters consider themselves deer hunters.

Deer hunting is attractive because the venison is excellent and the animal itself is wonderfully and vexingly difficult and challenging to hunt. However, as mentioned earlier, North America's whitetail herd alone may now be as large as thirty-six million. The population really snowballed in the 1960s and 1970s, with more than a dozen states suddenly claiming deer populations exceeding a million. This makes the whitetail deer the most populous large mammal (except for humankind) in the world. As wonderful as it is for the species, a population this large creates some problems for our own increasing population and our urban sprawl. We will discuss this in a later chapter, but for the current generation the white-tailed deer *is* the most available and accessible animal for the majority of American hunters. So, as naturally follows, American deer hunters are now the largest single-minded group of sports men and women in the world.

In the concrete jungles of our great cities it is difficult to understand what an important role deer hunting plays in the lifestyles of so many rural Americans (and urban dwellers who escape their cities when the season is open). We hunters are often asked whether we see a time when hunting may become a thing of the past. Clearly it will continue to change, but thanks to the white-tailed deer it is impossible to foresee such a sea change for so many Americans. Throughout much of rural America, school closures remain traditional when deer season opens, and the excitement, anticipation, and memories of deer seasons past, present, and future are not held exclusively by rural Americans. America is changing, and one change is that an increasing number of taxi drivers in major cities are now immigrants. Even so, to this day, in downtown Manhattan, if you happen to be stuck in traffic with an English-speaking cab driver, just ask about hunting, and for the rest of the ride you'll be regaled with tales of deer hunting in the Adirondacks.

The managing of our millions of deer—and the hunting culture our deer have spawned—will require a separate chapter. We can move on now with the prediction that it appears extremely unlikely that we would ever be able to manage our deer herds without hunting and equally unlikely that America's millions of deer hunters will become less avid and less dedicated.

Our white-tailed deer have proven both adaptable and prolific, with populations currently found in the entire lower forty-eight states, except for only California, Nevada, and perhaps Utah. They also occur across Canada and most of Mexico. However, in the West, whitetail populations are smaller and often sporadic, with mule deer and elk creating their own subcultures. Human populations are much less dense in the rural West, so hunter numbers are smaller but also tend to represent a larger percentage of the overall population. There is no hunting group in the world that compares to the number of whitetail hunters east of the Mississippi, but do not underestimate how equally avid Western deer and elk hunters are. This cannot so readily be seen in Los Angeles, San Francisco, Portland, Seattle, or even Denver and Phoenix, but outside the big cities hunting remains an important part of the lifestyle throughout the West.

There is a growing danger here because, as the cities continue to grow—and as more city dwellers retire and achieve their goal of moving into rural areas—Western hunters are decreasing as a percentage of the population and are slowly becoming disenfranchised. This is perhaps most easily seen in California, a state that is politically controlled by the three great cities of San Diego, Los Angeles, and San Francisco. To a lesser degree Denver and Colorado Springs are doing the same in Colorado, and Phoenix and Tucson in Arizona. This trend is changing the hunting culture of the American West, but it still remains strong. Outside of the great cities and despite the fact that hunters are being outvoted, hunting remains an important part of the lifestyle of the rural West, as it remains to the lifestyle of rural people in the Midwest and the South. Hunting is also an essential and equally unassailable management tool for our state and provincial wildlife agencies throughout North America.

By comparison hunting cultures elsewhere in the world are much, much smaller, although not necessarily less important. This has much to do with our North American model of wildlife management, as opposed to the system that developed in the Old World. In Europe hunting developed as the exclusive province of the landed gentry; part and parcel to the Robin Hood legend is that he became an outlaw—and hero—for poaching "the King's deer." In both Europe and North America hunters pay for wildlife management, but in Europe a much smaller number of hunters have become accustomed to paying much higher fees for the privilege than their American counterparts would be comfortable with.

Most modern European hunters are not of the old aristocracies, but they have grown up with a complex system of fees for animals taken based on sex, size, and age class, which in turn pays for game managers, called gamekeepers. Some who can afford it hold private hunting leases (as do Americans), but a major difference is that there is very little free access to public lands. This is a great luxury and privilege that American hunters enjoy, at least in part because, as a reactionary move against the European system left behind, our forefathers enabled vast tracts of public land for, literally, the public to enjoy.

This concept remains foreign to European hunters. However, they do have opportunities, and many European hunters are not wealthy. Often they band together as hunting clubs to secure leases. Game meat is customarily sold to defray costs (which is illegal and unthinkable in North America), and the privilege to take the small number of larger, older animals available in a given year might also be sold to visiting sports men and women willing to pay for the privilege. Although Europe has been settled for many centuries, there is actually a great deal of wildlife in most of the countries. This is the result of very careful management whereby wildlife is managed as a harvestable crop. A gamekeeper will customarily determine the number of animals that should be harvested—by sex and age class—to keep the herd healthy and within carrying capacity of the habitat. Many European hunters who are not wealthy or are unwilling to pay the fees for larger animals content themselves with harvesting management animals (which means animals that are not of trophy quality) or assisting in keeping the numbers of pests and predators under control.

European hunters not only tend to pay more for their hunting privileges than their American counterparts; they also generally work harder to attain and maintain that privilege. Obtaining a hunting license in Europe is a serious procedure that varies with the country but may take weeks or months of classroom work and fieldwork, culminating in both practical and written exams and a shooting test. In most countries European hunters are required to carry special insurance to hold a hunting license. With such stringent requirements, you can be assured that the European hunter jealously guards his or her privilege to hunt and takes pride in being a hunter. While overall numbers are small, the commitment made to be a hunter is generally recognized in European societies, along with the hunters' efforts in managing and maintaining wildlife populations. So the small minorities of European hunters tend to have the respect of the non-hunting majority, and they surely have earned it. France, Spain, Germany, Austria, and the Scandinavian countries all have significant hunting cultures, and all of these countries, despite high human populations, have tremendous wildlife resources.

Most of the rest of the world has tended toward the European model, with wildlife more or less "privatized," but we'll put that in quotes because the agency in control of the wildlife may be tribal or governmental. Things are quite different in developing countries, and it doesn't always work when we try to place Western values on societies that are still in basic survival mode. We need to keep in mind that the European system of game management that is so effective today has been developing for centuries. Our own North American model is a relatively new concept that has worked wonders for wildlife on our continent and has created the largest hunting culture the world has ever seen. It works for our hunters and it works for our wildlife, but it may not be exportable to other cultures throughout the world.

✢ Chapter Three ✢

American Hunters Today

While the majority of American hunters call themselves deer hunters, there are others—also totaling into the millions—who consider themselves duck hunters, pheasant hunters, turkey hunters, elk hunters, sheep hunters, or, perhaps more generically, big-game hunters and bird hunters.

There are other divisions as well. Hunters love challenge; that's part of the attraction. As modern firearms became more efficient, some individuals took steps backward, using by choice single-shot muzzleloaders like their grandfathers carried, which limited their range. Archery tackle is even more limiting, and its initial appeal was primarily the added challenge. However, as America's deer herds exploded and moved into areas of small farms and even suburbs, it was learned that muzzleloaders and especially bows and arrows, with much more limited range, could be used more safely than modern rifles in inhabited areas. At the same time, urged by growing numbers of hunters using such "primitive weapons," state game agencies recognized they could increase recreational opportunities and spread out hunting pressure by offering unique seasons for bow hunters and hunters using muzzleloaders.

Clearly this depends on the harvest goals for a given game species in a given area, but today it is common for there to be special archery seasons and muzzleloader seasons. So, while many hunters use multiple hunting tools and the true purists are in the minority, today there are sports men and women who consider themselves bow hunters or blackpowder hunters. Even these groups are often subdivided. Among the bow hunters are some who use only the traditional bare longbow. Others prefer the very sophisticated modern bow, with sights and cam wheels to increase velocity without increasing draw weight, and crossbows are also increasing in popularity. In the muzzleloading fraternity there are some who prefer original (or replica) side-hammer caplocks and flintlocks, and others who prefer the modern muzzleloader, with in-line ignition and, often, much better sights than our great granddads used. And there is also a relatively small but avid contingent of handgun hunters.

But, regardless of how they consider themselves, who are the modern American hunters? Are they the embodiment of Daniel Boone or Davy Crockett? Or are they the boorish slobs whom the anti-hunters paint them to be? In truth, they could be almost anyone! For one thing, as we have seen, the modern hunter doesn't have to be a "he." Historically, some very strong-minded women have overcome the male bias and become hunters, but it historically has been a sport that was overwhelmingly male dominated. It would be unrealistic to say that this has changed completely; there are still places where women will find it difficult to join the "boys club" of hunting. However, *this is changing*! As stated earlier, women comprise the fastest-growing group among hunters and are also the fastest-growing group of gun owners, purchasers of new firearms, and participants in both firearms and hunting-training programs.

Since hunting has long been a male-dominated pastime, most women are introduced by their spouses, boyfriends, and fathers, but today more male hunters are willing to make that introduction. Whether for better or worse, the traditional American family unit with two parents, 2.3 children, and 1.2 dogs is also changing, with more single-parent families than ever before. This can pose significant challenges for both young people and single moms who would like to hunt or at least learn more about hunting, but if there's enough will there is usually a way. So, in today's changing society, it isn't all that unusual for a single mom to introduce both sons and daughters to hunting, nor is it unusual to see single (and married) women joining both male and female buddies in the hunt. Today it still remains a little unusual for a female hunter to introduce a male partner to the sport, but that's only because the tremendous increase of women hunters is a fairly recent trend, so this will become much more commonplace as time goes on.

So much for sex. What about age? Well, it's an unfortunate truth that, as American's median age goes up, hunters are, on average, growing older. This is not just a function of the fact that people are living longer, so average ages are naturally increasing. Despite the millions of acres of public land available for all Americans to enjoy—and hunt on if we choose—our increasingly urban population and busy lifestyles make it more difficult for many people, and perhaps especially *young* people, to participate.

Numerous hunting, shooting, and conservation groups—and wildlife agencies—recognize this challenge and are making tremendous efforts to turn it around with special youth hunts, youth seasons, reduced license costs, mentoring and buddy programs, and more. We will discuss some of these opportunities in a later chapter. Right now, it's important to understand that hunting is an activity that not only can be enjoyed equally by men and women but also by people of all ages. Once again, how early depends on the person. It isn't uncommon for children to start with carefully supervised target shooting at the age of six or seven. The level of supervision required will decrease as the young person demonstrates sound judgment and safety habits, but whether a youngster should be turned loose in a deer stand at the age of seven or seventeen depends not just on the person but on how much practice, training, and supervised hunting he or she has received. Some states still have minimum age requirements (more frequently for big game than for birds and small game), and if so, the law is the law. The starting point really must be determined by the young person and his or her parent or mentor.

But here's part of the wonder of hunting: Regardless of when one starts, there really is no stopping point! It was mentioned earlier that the Boone and Crockett Club just held their twenty-eighth awards for North American big game. The hunters honored with recently taken trophies spanned the incredible age gap from eight years old to eighty! Howard R. French was honored for a fantastic pronghorn antelope that he took, literally, on his eightieth birthday! He was not, however, the oldest hunter to receive an award at this event. Trophies not previously measured for inclusion into the records can be recognized, and it was clear back in 1950 when Max Rasmussen took the largest mule deer buck of his life. In 2013 he was a spry ninety-three-year-old when he came onto the stage to receive his award.

Most hunting requires some level of physical activity, but some hunting situations are much more arduous than others. For safety, too, there is the requirement for some level of visual acuity. (That said, there are legally blind hunters who, with the assistance of a buddy to aim the firearm, are very successful and enjoy the experience every bit as much as a fully sighted person.) However, it's true that, sooner or later, the mountains are going to get a bit too steep and the tree-stand ladders a bit too high, but this depends entirely on the person. There is no mandatory retirement age among hunters. As when very young, an older hunter may need to enlist the assistance of a mentor, but here's another wonderful thing about hunting: It is not necessary to take game to savor the hunt. Older hunters are more likely to recognize this than youngsters, and as it becomes increasingly clear that autumns past outnumber autumns that lie ahead, just being in the woods and sharing a camp with friends and family becomes increasingly satisfying.

So hunters can't be defined by age any more than by sex. How about occupation or income bracket? Uh . . . no, that doesn't work very well, either. Hunters come from all walks of life, all creeds and colors, all religions, and all occupations. Many hunting camps are family affairs, and many others are composed of friends with similar backgrounds—one camp might be a group of doctors or lawyers and another might be factory workers or neighboring cattlemen. Most groups that *choose* to hunt together on a regular basis have some common ground. But there are many situations that are true melting pots.

Somewhere in the West, for instance, a national forest campground on the eve before opening day of elk season is a random group. Perhaps surprisingly, most camps on guided hunts are also random. Unless a group books the hunt together, there is no telling who one's camp-mates might be. So the heir to a textile fortune shares camp—and perhaps a tent—with a day laborer who has saved for three years to be there and the Christian with his or her Muslim campmate and the black hunter from the inner city with the white farmer from rural Georgia. The cultural and economic gaps can be huge, but the common ground is love of wildlife and passion for hunting—and that common ground will be found. Very rare exists the hunting camp where anyone is made to feel unwelcome on the basis of race, creed, culture, or social status. It just doesn't happen, because the common ground is too strong.

And here's another wonderful thing: Hunting is a great leveler. As with any activity, skill level matters. In hunting, things like physical condition, shooting skill, knowledge of the country and the game sought, and sheer *patience* count for much but are not enough to overcome imponderables like weather, game movement, and just plain luck. Whether you're sitting on a well-sited stand for a whitetail, glassing a mountainside for a ram, or walking a brushy fence line for a pheasant, the actual encounter is as much up to the animal as it is to you. The whitetail buck doesn't have to walk in view of your stand, the ram doesn't have to be on that particular mountain, and the pheasant doesn't have to be along that fence. None of these animals care how much money you have, what color you are, or who you pray to, and they also don't care how much experience you have or how much effort you have put into trying to arrange the encounter.

We call it beginner's luck because, despite everything, hunting success is random enough that beginners really do have a fair shot. But I've never heard it called expert's luck, or rich man's luck, or anything else. Not all hunting is free (and that's part of life, where few things are truly free), so there are situations whereby hunters in higher income brackets are more likely to be found. But once there, the hunting experience plays no favorites.

So, exactly where is that overweight, beer-swilling, foul-mouthed, male chauvinist pig hunter that the anti-hunters like to characterize as representing all hunters? Yes, he's there, too. The hunting community includes both sexes and all ages and walks of life, and while no people are truly better than others, some have better manners than others. It isn't possible to change one's upbringing, and to a degree we are products of our backgrounds. The manners, well . . . we can work on that. It's easy to accept that some hunters are very young, some are very old, and some have severe physical limitations. They're still our brother and sister hunters, and they're going to need some help. It isn't quite so easy to accept that there are hunters who aren't much fun to be around, especially if *you*, as a hunter, happen to be a lot different from that person.

But under the democracy of hunting (which, as we'll see later, isn't just a phrase but an actual tenet of our North American model of wildlife management), we may have to tolerate a little boorishness now and again, just as we tolerate the many differences among hunters and among people in our general society, provided, of course, that the person we are tolerating actually deserves the title of *hunter*. Here is one of the great lies the anti-hunters try to paint: First they create a caricature of a hunter as a most unpleasant monster. Such people do exist, but fortunately they are themselves becoming increasingly endangered not only in hunting but in the maturing of our society. Then, having painted that picture, they go on to paint a picture of this cartoon character laying waste to wildlife with wanton abandon. And this is where both hunters and non-hunters need to draw the line: Hunters pursue game *legally*, in accordance with the very complex system of hunting laws that *hunters created to regulate themselves* and thus *conserve wildlife for posterity*. Hunters adhere to seasons, bag limits, shooting hours, authorized methods of take, legal hunting areas, and so much more.

The personal appearance of hunters runs the full gamut, as do their personalities, but the *hunter* obeys the game laws that hunters who have gone before laid down so that our generation—and future generations—could continue to enjoy the hunt. This is a line that a person cannot cross and still claim to be, or expect to be called, a *hunter*. Fortunately we have another word that can be used to describe people who cross the line, who do not follow the game laws that, once again, were established *by* hunters and *for* hunters. We call these people *poachers*, and in fact they are not just petty criminals. They are thieves who are trying to steal the hunting heritage and resource that ethical and lawful hunters strive to conserve. The anti-hunters would paint us all with the same brush, but there are in fact *hunters*—millions of them. And, unfortunately, there are a very few *poachers*, whom genuine *hunters* must not tolerate in their midst.

✣ Chapter Four ✣

A Shameful Period

The European continent has been widely settled and more or less civilized for a thousand years, and yet in spite of its dense human population the European continent not only holds significant concentrations of wildlife but, amazingly, still has populations of almost all the large mammals that naturally developed there. The only real exception is the extinct aurochs, the wild ox once found across much of Eurasia. In the time of the Roman Empire the auroch was plentiful in France (known then as Gaul) and the forests of Germany and was heavily hunted for use in man-against-beast events in the Roman circus. Despite relentless persecution the last known aurochs persisted until 1637, but this is the only extinction in Europe that was clearly caused by modern humans.

Mind you, Europe was once quite a different place. There were cave bears, cave lions, mastodons, and more, and the northernmost subspecies of the African lion persisted in Greece until at least the fourth century BCE which, thanks to Herodotus and other scholars, lies within historic times. These animals are long gone, but in modern Europe the red deer, roe deer, and wild boar are widespread, occurring in virtually every country. Sweden, Finland, and the Baltic states have moose populations denser than anywhere in Canada or Alaska. Most European mountain ranges have significant populations of chamois, the small rock goat, and in more restrictive habitats there are several races of ibex. Wolves and the brown grizzly bear were indeed eradicated from much of Western Europe. However, both species remain plentiful in much of Eastern Europe and the remote forests of Scandinavia, and populations of both persist in Spain and the French Pyrenees.

Mind you, there have been some close calls. Both world wars were hard on Europe and hard on her wildlife. The European bison, or wisent, almost disappeared during World War II, but a remnant population in Poland was spared and this animal is no longer endangered. The magnificent Spanish ibex was very scarce in the years following the Spanish Civil War, but careful management has brought them back to plenty today. The European concept of hunting as the exclusive province of the aristocracy is foreign to Americans. But the historic evidence is that it worked in favor of Europe's wildlife and today's system of privatization and placing value on wildlife continues to work.

This is a far cry from what happened during the westward expansion of what is now the United States. In fact, the way we dealt with our wildlife from the beginning until the end of the nineteenth century is one of the most shameful chapters in our history. Wildlife was, of course, utilized for food from the time the first Europeans set foot in North America. Part of this attitude was reactionary. In direct contrast to the situation that many early immigrants left behind in Europe, in what seemed America's limitless wilderness, the common man could hunt for food. Later, it became a commonly held belief that wildlife and man could not coexist, so wildlife had to give way for agriculture and livestock.

It wasn't too long before Eastern populations of elk and bison vanished, and even deer became scarce in the original thirteen colonies. Even before the Revolution there were some minimal attempts to restrict the harvest, but on the one hand wildlife was considered an unlimited resource to be utilized, and on the other it seemed that wildlife needed to be eliminated to make way for the plow. Through the eighteenth century and on into the nineteenth, American wildlife was pushed ever westward or into sanctuary in the most inhospitable forests and swamps.

The destruction of the American bison is the best-known example of the excesses of the nineteenth century, but it is far from the only disaster that befell American wildlife. The wapiti, or American elk, was once widespread throughout much of the East, with the Eastern elk considered a unique subspecies, now extinct. It was this elk that Daniel Boone found in plenty when he first saw Kentucky in the fall of 1767, but by then elk were already scarce in the colonies to the east. Elk disappeared from South Carolina in 1737; North Carolina, in the 1780s; New York, in 1847; Virginia, in 1855; and Pennsylvania, in 1858. The last known Eastern elk were exterminated in Minnesota and Missouri in the late 1890s. By this time wildlife was faring equally poorly in the American West. The Merriam's subspecies of elk, originally found in New Mexico and Arizona, is believed to have become extinct in 1906.

Also lost was the badlands, or Audubon's, bighorn, named in honor of early naturalist John James Audubon. This was the bighorn of the breaks and badlands of eastern Wyoming and Montana and western Nebraska and the Dakotas. It was this bighorn sheep that George Armstrong Custer hunted on his Black Hills expedition in 1874 and that Theodore Roosevelt hunted during his sojourn in the West in 1884 to 1886. This race of bighorn became extinct in 1905.

As with the lost races of elk, unrestricted hunting is generally given as the cause, and this is probably correct. But disease also could have been a factor. We know now that wild sheep are especially susceptible to diseases carried by domestic sheep, so disease could have been a greater issue than the settlers' rifles. Either way, these animals were lost forever at the hands of humans. Today tens of thousands of elk roam the country once occupied by Merriam's elk, and smaller herds have been reestablished in numerous areas in the East. Regrettably, these are not the original species but are introduced Rocky Mountain elk. Similarly, bands of introduced Rocky Mountain bighorns now occupy much of the habitat where the badlands bighorn once roamed. These introductions constitute just a few of the many great North American conservation success stories, but what a shame these original species were lost, as were the passenger pigeon and the heath hen.

The Eastern and Merriam's elk and the badlands bighorn seem almost forgotten. Forgotten, too, is that elk and pronghorn antelope once roamed the Great Plains in untold numbers and were preyed upon by wolves and grizzly bears. Remembered is what happened to the bison, perhaps the most shameful and most classic American example of human's excesses.

It is not clear today that the Eastern bison was a distinct subspecies, but when European humans first set foot on the North American continent there were some bison in the Eastern woodlands. They vanished quickly, as did the bison Daniel Boone found in the wilderness west of the Cumberland Gap. How widespread or numerous bison might have been in the East is not known today, but it is known that the great numbers lay in the West, with a primary range stretching across the Great Plains from the Texas panhandle to southern Canada. It is estimated that there might have been sixty million bison roaming the plains at some point in the mid-nineteenth century. Trade in buffalo robes had been conducted for decades, but the effect was small because of limited access to the primary markets in the East. On May 10, 1869, a golden spike was hammered, signaling the completion of America's transcontinental railroad. That spike also went into the coffins of millions of American bison.

With rail access to both the Eastern and growing California markets the demand for bison robes grew, and buffalo runners flocked to the plains. The profligate waste was amazing. Some meat, especially in winter, was sped to the railhead, and buffalo tongues, a delicacy of the day, were pickled and brined. But the majority of the carcasses were left to rot on the plains, and when it was all over bone collectors gathered the skeletons to be ground up as fertilizer. It didn't last long. The whole thing is shocking by today's standards. It is absolutely true that passengers on trains potted bison just to pass the time. None of this has any relationship to modern sport hunting, nor do modern hunters condone such butchery.

However, it must be understood that this happened in a different time from now and the slaughter was politically motivated as well as economically. By 1874 the great Kansas herds were already depleted, and in that year President Grant pocket vetoed a bill passed by Congress to save the bison. A year later General Phil Sheridan stood before Congress imploring the destruction of the bison as the best means to pacify the plains tribes. The bison were indeed part and parcel to the way of life of numerous tribes, including what were considered troublesome groups, such as the Comanche in the south and the Sioux and Cheyenne in the north. The bison herds were their larder, and, especially after the Custer fight in 1876, part of America's so-called manifest destiny was that the bison had to go.

By then the handwriting was already on the wall. By 1874 the Kansas herds were too diminished for commercial hunting to pay, so the buffalo runners turned south into Oklahoma and the Texas panhandle. In the late 1880s the great zoologist, naturalist, and hunter William Temple Hornaday

(1854–1937), then chief taxidermist for the United States National Museum, researched the demise of the bison. Based on firsthand accounts, he concluded that the southern herds of Kansas, Oklahoma, and Texas had become extinct in 1876. The runners then turned north, annihilating the bison in Wyoming, the Dakotas, and finally Montana. The last viable commercial season took place in the winter of 1883–1884, and afterward only scattered survivors remained.

In 1886 Hornaday was tasked to secure specimens for the museum so future generations would know what bison looked like. He found small herds on the Musselshell River in eastern Montana, but in that year he wrote, "The extermination of the large herds of buffalo in the United States is already an accomplished fact." Fortunately there were a few remnants here and there, including a herd of about two hundred in what is now Yellowstone National Park. Hornaday is given and deserves much credit for saving the bison from extinction—almost after the fact—but, like so many Americans of his day, until almost too late he was a proponent of the concept that the bison must go.

Although a shameful event in American history, the destruction of the bison may not have been as simple or straightforward as it sounds. We tend to credit a few hundred—possibly a very few thousand—commercial hunters with eliminating sixty million bison, but it probably didn't happen exactly like that. In 1870 the U.S. human population was 38.5 million; by 1880 we had swollen to fifty million. Either way, this represents a buffalo robe for every man, woman, and child, with millions to spare! The records of buffalo hides shipped by rail, even if inflated to account for missing or incomplete documents, barely reached 1.5 million.

The oft-quoted figure of sixty million bison has been stated for so long that we accept it as an article of faith, but this (or any other) estimate may or may not have validity. The figure of sixty million bison was apparently first proposed by respected naturalist Ernest Thompson Seton (1860–1946), who, like Hornaday, made his determinations after the great herds were gone but when firsthand accounts were still available. So the real number will never be known, but it seems likely today that the bison population actually peaked in about 1845, following a long period of good rains and thus good grass on the prairies. The next fifteen years saw extended drought on the Great Plains, and it appears that bison numbers may have dropped considerably before the commercial hunting started to have significant effects. Hornaday's own estimate is that fifteen million bison remained in 1867, still a very large number but much different from sixty million.

College professor and outdoor writer Dr. Sam Fadala recently did some research on this subject. Hard data are scarce. The actual number of commercial bison hunters is totally unknown, and very few left written accounts probably because many of them were illiterate. Fadala's conclusions (published in *Petersen's HUNTING* magazine and available on the Internet) are that, although the carnage was terrible, the shooting of all the bison "never happened." His premise is that, given the logistics involved and the weaponry available, the natural increase of the however-many-millions of bison should have offset the worst destruction the buffalo runners were able to inflict. Clearly the commercial hunters didn't help, nor did the thrill killers shooting from trains, but he believes the most likely real culprit was disease. The sheer numbers game supports this, plus a few period accounts of large numbers of bison found dead, not skinned and apparently not shot. There is also the simple fact that domestic livestock pushed West with the settlers, and the unsophisticated bison could have been extremely susceptible to bovine disease.

Please accept that this is not given in mitigation of or apology for the excesses of the nineteenth century. Regardless of exactly how it happened, the near-extinction of the bison is a sad and true story. But this is a story most of us know about and attribute to "hunters," in quotes because neither the commercial buffalo runners nor the murderers were hunters as modern sports men and women wish to be known and the real story may be more complex than history chose to record.

The story that is much less known is that, while the bison is a showcase example, there was much, much more, and perhaps worse. The bison is a very large animal. If there were millions of them on the plains, then how many pronghorns, elk, and deer might there have been, with little or no commercial value? Kansas, center of the Great Plains and typified by open country where large mammals are vulnerable, is almost unique in declaring deer extinct, but before the last deer vanished the pronghorns, elk, grizzly bears, and wolves were all long gone along with the bison. The great bastions of the Western mountains provided a last refuge for many species, as did the deepest swamps and thickest forests of most Eastern states. But by the end of the nineteenth century the destruction of America's wildlife was almost complete. Fortunately the long road back had already begun.

✣ CHAPTER FIVE ✣

Introductions and Reintroductions

By 1900 most populations of North America's large mammals were in trouble and existed only in isolated populations. Perhaps a thousand bison survived, the majority being in Canada or in small captive herds. White-tailed deer still numbered about a half million, certainly not endangered, but a small shadow of the millions that had roamed North America a century earlier. Elk had been reduced to perhaps forty thousand, pronghorns to about five thousand, and wild turkeys to fewer than one hundred thousand. The very survival of all these (and other) species seemed in question, and throughout the contiguous United States most wildlife populations were mere remnants of what they had been.

Fortunately a handful of forward-thinking Americans understood that the plains would be even lonelier without pronghorns, the fall forests quieter without the bugling of bull elk, and the spring woods a boring place without the gobbling of a wild turkey. In 1887 Theodore Roosevelt and like-minded friends founded the Boone and Crockett Club, and they deserve much credit for starting that long road back. There were bumps along that road, but the results today are amazing and a victory all North Americans should celebrate. No matter what the peak was, never again will bison roam in the tens of millions, nor could farmers and ranchers tolerate such numbers. But today there are nearly a half million of the great shaggy beasts, so clearly their future is secure. Elk have increased to about 1.4 million, pronghorns to over a million. Today elk are more creatures of the high country than they are of the plains and badlands, but pronghorns are now a common sight along the interstates across much of the Great Plains. The current estimate of white-tailed deer runs as high as thirty-six million, and wild turkeys, too, number well into the millions.

In some cases the remnant populations simply needed protection to recover. Given closed seasons and very selective hunting—and good habitat—wildlife is amazingly resilient and over time will creep out of the mountains and forests and reoccupy their former range. This was true of many of our whitetail populations and certainly our remaining elk populations in the northern Rockies. But a wildlife population that is *gone* is an altogether different story: The good (but empty) habitat remained, but where might animals come from? In the early 1900s America's conservation movement had opportune timing: A good rail network had already been established, and motorized vehicles were coming into use. In general our wildlife was in serious trouble, but North America is a big place and there were reserves we could draw on. For key Western species, such as elk, our great Yellowstone National Park, created by President Grant in 1872, became a key reservoir.

Named after naturalist Clinton Hart Merriam (1855–1942), the Merriam's elk of the Southwestern United States became extinct in 1906 from unregulated hunting. The Merriam's elk vanished so quickly and utterly that significant differences between it and the Rocky Mountain elk to the north aren't entirely clear, but it is recognized as a separate and now-vanished species of elk. From the wisdom of a century later, now it is clearly preferable that protection had come a decade earlier, in time to save this animal. But history is unforgiving, extinction is forever, and timing is everything.

Merriam's elk were gone for only a few years before the introduction of Rocky Mountain elk from Yellowstone began. In 1911 a small number of Yellowstone elk were introduced into New Mexico's Sangre de Cristo Mountains. In 1913 Arizona chapters of the Elks Club brought seventy-nine Yellowstone elk into northern Arizona. They were offloaded at Winslow, and although other releases followed, these elk formed the nucleus of the great herds that now roam in both states. These northern elk seemed to have little problem in the southerly mountains. Numbers built up quickly, and in 1935 Arizona held its first modern (and legal) elk season. Readers with any exposure to hunting literature might be interested to know that Jack O'Connor, then a young English professor at the University of Arizona—and for the next forty years America's "dean of outdoor writers"—participated in that inaugural 1935 elk hunt.

Yellowstone elk have been responsible for the establishment of new elk herds all over the West and also in the East, with this effort continuing to this day. Technically, placing Rocky Mountain elk into the Southwest's former Merriam's elk range and into states such as Pennsylvania, Minnesota, Michigan, Wisconsin, Tennessee, Kentucky, and West Virginia and the former range of the Eastern elk (also extinct) would be called an introduction. These areas were elk country but not the country of *that* exact elk! Establishment of herds into the Great Plains states—Kansas, Nebraska, Oklahoma, the Dakotas—is properly termed *reintroduction* because as far as we know the original elk were probably of the Rocky Mountain variety. But however you define it, the early establishment of Yellowstone National Park saved a large population of elk that, for more than a century, have been trapped and relocated and have created the wonderful elk populations that exist today. Historically this great effort was conducted by government agencies and private individuals and groups. Today it is still ongoing, but the Rocky Mountain Elk Foundation takes the lead.

Bighorn sheep, now considered creatures of the high mountains, were once nearly as common in the foothills and badlands as elk and pronghorns were on the plains. Although all wild game was prized by hungry settlers, the meat of the wild sheep is considered some of the best, and that was surely a problem. But wild sheep have another, larger problem, and that is extreme vulnerability to diseases carried by domestic livestock. Even into the 1960s America's bighorn sheep were dwindling, but careful management and innumerable introductions and reintroductions have brought them back. Today this effort is led by the Wild Sheep Foundation. Because of the disease issue wild sheep are fragile, and there have been bumps in the road. But today healthy wild sheep populations exist in all the Western states and also in the breaks of Nebraska and the Dakotas.

By 1920 wild turkeys were altogether gone from eighteen of the thirty-nine states believed to have held native populations. It took decades to reestablish populations, and the state wildlife agencies have become very clever about this by trading turkeys for elk, deer for turkeys, and so forth. Today turkey conservation efforts are led by the National Wild Turkey Federation, working with the state and provincial wildlife agencies, and we have turkeys not only north to south but also coast to coast. This is saying quite a bit because the wild turkey's current range far exceeds its original limits. For instance, wild turkeys are now found across southern Canada, far north of their original range, and are well established in California, which historically held no turkeys at all.

There are actually four species of wild turkey in the United States, with distinct feathering, plus a couple more in Mexico. Although all wild turkeys were getting scarce at one time, none of the species were seriously endangered, so in most cases the wildlife agencies were able to reintroduce turkeys of the original, native breed. But as populations expand there has been some "bumping together" that perhaps never occurred in nature. From Texas to Oklahoma and Kansas there is now an intergrade area in which Eastern and Rio Grande turkeys come together as natural hybrids but created by man's aggressive reestablishment of dwindling populations.

Farther west and north, in Nebraska and the Dakotas, Eastern birds bump against the Western Merriam's species (also named for Clinton Hart Merriam). In California, well . . . the Golden State wasn't native turkey country, and in getting the birds started the game department took turkeys where they could get them. The majority of birds are primarily Rio Grande stock, but there were Merriam's turkeys introduced at higher elevations and a few Eastern birds as well. So California has "wild turkeys," but their race is a bit difficult to establish!

To some extent the same thing happened with white-tailed deer. Much of the expansion and explosion of the whitetail has been totally natural, but in some areas both wildlife departments and private individuals jump-started the process by bringing in whitetails from elsewhere (Southern states that still had a lot of turkeys often traded turkeys for whitetails). This was a good thing, but it also complicated the situation somewhat. You see, there are dozens of subspecies of white-tailed deer, differing slightly in color but mostly in size. The whitetails of the Deep South are, naturally, considerably smaller than are those of the northern woods race of the Upper Midwest. But, a generation or two back, when Southern whitetails were still scarce, the occasional truckload of Wisconsin whitetails found their way into Georgia.

So, has this messed things up? From a purely scientific point of view, you bet; there are a lot of gene pools that are no longer purely the original stock. From a layperson's point of view, it's wonderful to have deer and turkeys in the woods. And hunters in southern Georgia aren't likely to complain if their deer are somewhat bigger than the deer in adjacent Alabama, South Carolina, or Florida.

This is, however, a good example of the myriad ways that humans have altered the natural world, and, in some cases, it's almost impossible to determine exactly what the natural order of things actually should have been. This business of introducing and reintroducing animals is hardly new and certainly not unique to North America. The fallow deer is an attractive and oddly tractable deer that has been moved around since Roman times, so much so that we aren't exactly certain what its original range might have been, although Mesopotamia—modern-day Iraq east into Iran—is probably a reasonable guess. George Washington had fallow deer as ornamentation on his Mount Vernon estate, and today free-range fallow deer populations can be found on all continents except Antarctica. Similarly, mouflon sheep have been so widely introduced that the actual origin and original range of "European mouflon" is also uncertain, although Corsica, Sardinia, Cyprus, and perhaps the Adriatic coastline are pretty good guesses. Today there are quite a few free-range mouflon (and hybrids with domestic sheep) in Texas, and there are isolated populations of free-range fallow deer here and there in the United States.

Some human-caused introductions, whether inadvertent or on purpose, have proven disastrous. The kudzu plant is a scourge in the American South, as is prickly pear in South Africa. The brown snake threatens Guam's bird life, and feral donkeys are a plague on cattle and sheep stations in Western Australia. Feral populations of pigs, goats, and primitive domestic sheep were established in many areas by early seafarers wishing to establish a ready meat source for passing ships; in other areas feral populations were established by local practices of allowing livestock to run free. By whatever cause, feral animals have often bred up to nuisance proportions, especially in limited habitats, such as on California's Channel Islands.

It isn't just a matter of domestic animals. Fallow deer and mouflon are the oldest known examples, but man has been moving "wild" animals around for centuries. In both New Zealand and Australia the majority of the large mammals were introduced, in some cases as meat sources (water buffalo and banteng in Australia's Northern Territories) and in other cases simply because a seemingly empty landscape needed filling with species familiar to the settlers (as in red stag in New Zealand). In more recent times some experimentation has had its basis in science. The late Frank Hibben (1910–2002) was a well-known archaeologist, writer, big-game hunter, and winner of the prestigious Weatherby Hunting and Conservation Award. Hibben had a theory about habitat niches seemingly unfilled by native species, and during his tenure as chairman of the New Mexico Game and Fish Commission, between 1961 and 1971, he experimented with several nonnative introductions.

Persian ibex were introduced into the Florida Mountains; Siberian ibex, into the Canadian River canyon; gemsbok or giant oryx (a large desert antelope from southern Africa), into the White Sands area; and aoudad or Barbary sheep, here and there. The Siberian ibex apparently vanished, but the other species have done very well. Only the Persian ibex in the Floridas are known to have caused habitat problems; like most goats, they are voracious as well as prolific, and periodically their numbers have required substantial reduction.

This was a half century ago. Today wildlife biologists are much more aware of the potential downsides to both native flora and fauna from introducing nonnative species and also to the difficulty of getting the genie back in the bottle if necessary! California's Channel Islands are a prime and very sad example. Most of these islands had out-of-control feral pig populations, established by passing ships under Spanish rule. Santa Catalina and San Clemente had feral goats; Santa Cruz had feral sheep. Santa Rosa had too many pigs, but it also had a wonderful herd of Roosevelt's elk from the Olympic Peninsula and an equally wonderful herd of mule deer from the Kaibab, both introduced by the island's owner in the early years of the twentieth century. The Nature Conservancy, a private group generally neutral on the subject of hunting, acquired Santa Rosa, with a charter to turn it over to the government as part of the Channel Islands National Park.

So far so good, except that the long-term plan was to return the islands to "pre-European man." It took a lot of money and helicopter time, but the feral pigs, sheep, and goats were eradicated throughout much of the Channel Islands, including the destruction of an estimated twelve thousand pigs on Santa Rosa, which left a herd of perhaps twelve hundred elk and twenty-five hundred mule deer, controlled and apparently well managed by a guided hunting program. Time and again, the deer and elk on Santa Rosa received a stay of execution, but the end was always in sight.

There is no question but that the long-overpopulated hogs did serious damage to the island. There was little evidence, if any, of long-term habitat destruction by deer or elk. It seemed unthinkable that the liberal voters of California would stand by and allow the destruction of these wonderful herds of elk and mule deer, but the unthinkable happened. In 2011 both populations were wiped out by aerial gunning, the carcasses left to rot. The biological necessity of such waste isn't comprehensible, but it serves as a caution to introduction of nonindigenous species.

Of course, Roosevelt's elk and Rocky Mountain mule deer are not endangered species. One wonders whether the National Park Service would have been so quick with the helicopter gunships had the island been instead populated by an endangered species? Perhaps not, but many introductions have been based on availability rather than on other concerns, such as conserving a species becoming scarce in its native land. New Mexico's state-sponsored experiments are an ideal example. Neither Persian nor Siberian ibex are rare in their native lands, so what a shame that they didn't experiment with Nubian ibex from the Red Sea Hills or Walia ibex from Ethiopia's Simien Plateau. Gemsbok remain extremely plentiful in southern Africa, but scimitar oryx from Africa's Sahara region are more or less extinct in the wild. They would have done equally well.

Hindsight is 20/20, but foresight rarely is. However, some introductions have been so successful that many people tend to forget the species isn't native. The ring-necked Chinese pheasant is one of America's most popular game birds, now existing in tens of millions across a huge range. The first pheasants known to arrive in the United States landed in Washington's Olympic Peninsula in 1881 and were released into Oregon's Willamette Valley. It's thought that this first introduction didn't take, but further introductions were made in 1882 and 1884, and before long Oregon had America's first breeding population of pheasant. Some spread naturally, but mostly the range was expanded by on-purpose releases, and today the pheasant is an important game bird and resource in several dozen states.

Although the pheasant doesn't naturally belong in North America, it is rarely argued that it is a detriment to native species. This cannot be said of another incredibly successful and much more inadvertent introduction: the feral hog. Although some conscious introductions of wild European stock have been made, in general North America's feral hog populations are simply that: domestic hogs that, left to roam free, have turned wild. Feral hog populations have existed here and there for hundreds of years. On the one hand they're a disaster. They dig up the ground with their rooting, they raid crops, and they probably displace native wildlife. On the other hand, they're here, they aren't going away, and today they are rapidly expanding their range. Mostly they're bad news, except, from a hunter's standpoint, they are offering wonderfully expanding hunting opportunity. Also, they're really good to eat!

Between these two extremes, and largely through luck, a number of species have been conserved—or saved for better days—by introductions into nonnative ranges. Zoos have been and are a very important part of this process, but because of space limitations the most that the world's zoological gardens can generally offer is insurance against extinction. Private herds can bolster this insurance and, over time, can generate the numbers for reintroduction back into native ranges when and if conditions allow. Although these species are not considered endangered, these are simple facts: There are more blackbuck antelope and axis deer in Texas than in all of their native Indian subcontinent and more aoudad in the American Southwest than in North Africa.

These three, together with fallow deer, mouflon, and European red deer, are probably the world's most common exotic, or nonnative, introduced large mammal species. Sika deer and Himalayan tahr also occur on multiple continents. Actually, we have moved animals around so much that there's "stuff" all over the place. Publishing magnate William Randolph Hearst introduced quite a variety of species onto his San Simeon (California) estate in the 1920s. Today there are established populations of aoudad, Himalayan tahr, and sambar free ranging along the Central Coast, and once in a while local ranchers complain about zebras breaking fences.

In the mid-nineteenth century the Duke of Bedford introduced a number of species onto his Woburn Abbey estate, northwest of London. As the story goes, during a storm the brick wall was breached and some animals escaped. Exactly what isn't known is at least two varieties of escapees persisted: Chinese water deer, a really interesting Asian deer with no antlers and huge Dracula-like fangs, developed a free-range population in that part of England. The muntjac did even better. Another petite Asian deer with pixie-like antlers and somewhat smaller fangs, the muntjac is now believed to be the island's most plentiful game animal, having surpassed the native (and very common) roebuck.

It should be obvious that a lot of the long-standing introductions were done not exactly for conservation but out of curiosity or, to put it bluntly, by landowners who introduced exotic species simply because they could. Obviously a certain interest in wildlife was required but also the wherewithal. Most of the many nonnative species present in Texas were introduced in a time when gas and oil were booming and cattle prices were high. But for whatever reason, introduced species have filled the very real function of saving numerous species that have been lost on native range.

The most classic case of all is probably Pere David's deer, a primitive antlered Chinese deer that was extinct in the wild, with the last herd found in the Emperor's private garden near Peking. Father Armand David, a French missionary to China, made Western science aware of this deer in 1866, and apparently he smuggled a few specimens to Europe. In 1900 the Emperor's small herd was killed and eaten during the Boxer Rebellion. After the species' extinction in China, Herbrand Russell, eleventh Duke of Bedford, acquired all the specimens he could find in European zoos and moved them to Woburn Abbey, where they thrived. Woburn Abbey still has a large herd, with surplus sent around the world. Pere David's deer are now found in small private herds in Texas, Argentina, and South Africa and once again in China. Starting in 1985 there have been several reintroductions from the Woburn Abbey herd into China, with the Chinese population now about three thousand in several well-guarded reserves.

In the United States, Texas is the center of the exotic ranching industry. There's no telling what you might find on a ranch in Texas! In some cases (the African eland is one example) nonnative species were experiments in alternative meat production; in other cases the releases were vanity based, purely ornamental. The Schreiner family of the YO Ranch are credited with making the shocking discovery that (at least some) hunters were just crazy enough to actually pay for a crack at one of those strange nonnative beasts. Hunting placed value on the introduced species, and an industry was born, not just hunting, but buying, selling, and trading breeding stock.

Regardless of your position on hunting, this almost has to be an acceptable concept. As mentioned, the most common exotics are not endangered at home, although they may be more plentiful elsewhere. But the Texas exotics ranching industry has created significant populations of animals that *are* *endangered* on their native ranges. These include Eld's deer and barasingha (both Asian deer), plus Bukharan markhor, plus, well, a whole bunch of other species. The Arabian oryx was almost extinct in the wild when Arabian oryx from herds in the United States were reintroduced into the Arabian Peninsula. Many other species exist in small, scattered, and thus genetically diverse private herds in North America, just waiting for better times to make reintroductions into native range practical.

So, here is the strange case of the "three amigos." These are three African antelope that have been established in significant breeding populations in the United States (primarily in Texas): scimitar or white oryx, addax, and Dama gazelle. As a group they have several things in common. Although size and horn configurations vary, all are very pale to best reflect the harsh sun of the Sahara Desert, which is their native ground. Perhaps more to the point, all are extinct (or very close to it) on native range, so as was the case with Pere David's deer, captive herds now in existence are the only hope for these species.

They are, of course, and properly on CITES Appendix I (endangered) and on the U.S. endangered species list, so if a pocket should be discovered somewhere in the vastness of the North African desert it could not be exploited. But U.S. Fish and Wildlife allowed an exception for trade in breeding stock and hunting of privately owned herds in the United States because this obviously placed value on the animals and was beneficial to all three species. There are thousands of scimitar oryx in Texas. Addax and Dama gazelle are less common, but all three are found on numerous Texas ranches.

Then came insanity. The Friends of Animals sued U.S. Fish and Wildlife, demanding that all trade in these "endangered species" be curtailed or at least be conducted in full compliance with our Endangered Species Act. They won, and in the window between the judgment and implementation a fire sale took place, with numerous ranchers unloading their stock of these animals out of concern that they would have no value and they would be stuck with them. This is not exactly a "law of unintended consequences" issue. Priscilla Feral, President of the Friends of Animals, actually stated on national television (a *60 Minutes* interview) that she would rather these species be extinct than hunted, which pretty much encapsulates the challenge hunters and wildlife managers alike face when attempting to deal with *serious* anti-hunters.

The good news is that the current situation has stabilized. There is a permit process by which a landowner is allowed to sell or harvest surplus animals, and U.S. Fish and Wildlife has been prompt and receptive in handling that process. So, despite the worst intentions of America's anti-hunters, the three amigos still exist in breeding herds in the United States, they still have value, and they're still available for a more peaceful time when reintroductions can be made across the southern Sahara.

CHAPTER SIX

The North American Model

P rior to the American Revolution some of the thirteen colonies enacted rudimentary game laws. In some cases the intent was cultural rather than to truly protect a resource. A good example is the "no hunting on Sunday" law, which persists in some states and provinces to this day, despite our increasingly secular societies, ever more hectic lives, and the simple fact that, in America today, our ethnic mix has changed and millions of people celebrate the Sabbath on days other than Sunday. Some, however, were intended to conserve an already dwindling resource: Massachusetts attempted to enforce a closed season on deer (with strict penalties) prior to 1700. In the main, however, utilization of our wildlife resources was a free-for-all through most of the nineteenth century.

In part this was a reactionary response to the European societies left behind, where from feudal times wildlife belonged to the landed gentry. Common people, no matter how hungry, were rarely able to legally hunt. Part, too, was the doctrine of Manifest Destiny, which decreed it was the God-given and inevitable right for the United States to expand westward all the way to the Pacific, conquering all the wild lands, wild animals, and peoples that blocked the way. This last included not only the indigenous tribes but also other colonial powers (remembering that California and much of the Southwest were already claimed by Mexico).

Despite the major roadblocks that lay ahead, by the early 1800s, and especially following the epic Lewis and Clark expedition, Americans knew that a vast continent lay before them. Our pioneers knew that the new lands to the West were far different from long-settled Europe. Different, too, was that there were no kings and no nobles, a concept their fathers and grandfathers had fought a long and costly war to be rid of. So there would be no "crown land." Indeed there was plenty of land for the taking, and for a time its supply seemed inexhaustible, as well as the supply of wild creatures inhabiting the untamed land.

The way in which American wildlife resources are managed, conserved, and appropriately utilized to this day actually has its basis in English common law, with the major difference that the mandate of the elected government replaces the prerogative of royalty. Although another generation would pass before we got serious about wildlife conservation, the most basic tenet of North American wildlife management stems from the U.S. Supreme Court ruling in the case of *Martin v. Waddell* in 1842. The case was actually a dispute about the rights to an oyster fishery in New Jersey's Raritan River, but the court decision established the keystone of the wildlife management doctrine that we follow and hold dear to this day, namely that wildlife is owned by no one but is held in trust by the government for the benefit of all the people.

In his ruling Chief Justice Roger Taney wrote, "When the people of New Jersey took possession of the reins of government, and took into their own hands the powers of sovereignty, the prerogatives and regalities which before belonged to either the crown or the parliament, became immediately and rightly vested in the state." Later Supreme Court rulings upheld and built upon this doctrine, over time validating, as Justice White wrote in 1896, that the states had the "right to control and regulate the common property in game," with such control exercised "as a trust for the benefit of the people."

The situation in Canada was similar in some ways but different in others. Canadian pioneers faced an even greater vastness of wilderness, consumed and still occupied by a much smaller human population—but they eventually faced the same problem of rapidly diminishing wildlife. Canada fought no war to rid themselves of the British crown. On July 1, 1867 (still celebrated as "Dominion Day"), the Dominion of Canada was created as a self-governing entity within the British Empire, and so it remains today. One small result of this is that government, or public land, in Canada is still referred to as crown land. However, the Canadian system of wildlife management is almost identical to our own, and numerous wildlife-related treaties bind the two countries.

Mexico had a bit later start than its neighbors to the north because of invasions by the United States in 1846 and France in 1861 and its own civil war started in 1910 and lasted until 1929. Even so, Mexico's system of hunting seasons, licensing, and wildlife management is increasingly similar to ours and Canada's, although understandably perhaps a generation behind. So it truly is appropriate for us to refer to the way we manage, conserve, and utilize our wildlife resources not as U.S.-based model but as the North American Model of Wildlife Conservation.

As stated by The Wildlife Society, an organization of eleven thousand wildlife professionals, there are seven focal points to our North American model. First and foremost is the keystone: **wildlife as public trust resources**. No one owns wildlife; it is in the public trust. Somewhat uniquely compared to much of the rest of the world, this applies to wildlife on private land as well as on public land. In practice, a landowner can choose to utilize wildlife on his or her land or not, but if the choice is made to hunt or fish (or allow others to) then these activities may be conducted only in accordance with public law. The concept that all people own American wildlife and that it is held in trust and managed by our elected governments is the single most important concept in American wildlife management. It became the driving force of our wonderful wildlife recovery through the twentieth century and is a major factor in the amazing plenty we enjoy today.

Elimination of markets for game. This is also a bit unusual compared to other continents but is almost certainly a direct result of the abuses of the nineteenth century and on into the twentieth. It is generally illegal to sell wildlife. There are some obvious exceptions. Commercial fishing is conducted under vastly different laws from sportfishing, and furbearers, whether hunted or trapped, are also generally under different licensing regulations. But, for instance, if you see venison on a restaurant menu in the United States you can assume correctly that the meat came from a farmed animal raised for the table. In Europe, where game meat is very popular, "venison" in a restaurant may well have come from a red deer harvested a mile away—or it might have been shipped frozen from Argentina or New Zealand.

Allocation of wildlife by law. Generally speaking game laws have evolved as the jurisdiction of the states and provinces, which certainly makes sense because conditions in Maine are much different from those in Nevada. There are, however, federal mandates (such as the Endangered Species Act) that supersede state jurisdiction. Migratory species, such as waterfowl, also receive more general federal protection and management. All of us, and most especially ethical hunters, value game laws with teeth because poachers are stealing wildlife from all of us. One of the toothiest we have is the Lacey Act. Originally drafted to stop trafficking in birds, the Lacey Act makes it a U.S. federal violation to conduct interstate or international traffic in illegally taken wildlife. So, if you poach a deer in Iowa you will be prosecuted by the local authorities. But if you take that illegal deer across the state line into Missouri, you have just violated the Lacey Act, which generally carries far more severe penalties. Similarly, if Americans should break a game law while hunting in Canada, they are subject to local sanctions, but if they bring an illegally taken animal back into the United States they have just violated the Lacey Act and can be prosecuted in federal court. Specific game laws vary considerably from place to place, so it is important for hunters to be conscious of the local game laws wherever they are hunting.

Wildlife should be killed only for a legitimate purpose. As mentioned earlier, many rural people throughout North America rely heavily upon game meat to augment their diets, which is certainly a legitimate purpose. However, edible game meat should *always* be utilized, and in North American society the choice between game and genuine starvation is fairly rare. The most critical criteria that defines "legitimate purpose" is that there is a harvestable surplus, that the harvest is sustainable, that the wildlife taken is utilized, and that hunting of a given species in a given area is beneficial to the management of that species in that area.

Wildlife is considered an international resource. We in North America are the stewards of our wildlife, held in the public trust and administered by our elected governments. However, the wildlife of the United States, Canada, and Mexico is not owned solely by the peoples of our country but are in turn held in trust for the world. This tenet stems from migratory bird treaties with Canada in the early years of the twentieth century (and later with Mexico) and continues with major North American involvement in international initiatives, such as the international treaty known as CITES—the Convention on International Trade in Endangered Species—and the international ban on ivory trade. Considering wildlife an international resource places an even heavier burden of responsibility on wise management.

Science is the proper tool for discharge of wildlife policy. Wildlife management is not always perfect science. Despite the best intentions, a bad winter or a prolonged drought can have disastrous effects, as can overpopulation in a succession of good years. Diseases come and go in wild populations, and there often isn't any solution but to let them run their course. In the summer of 2012 the very fatal EHD, epizootic hemorrhagic disease, often called "blue tongue," swept through the whitetail herds in much of the Upper Midwest, decimating the population. Such things are usually as impossible to predict as to stop. So there's nothing easy or simple about sound wildlife management, but the professional wildlife managers and biologists at local, state, and federal levels do the best job they can, and in the past hundred years have wrought genuine miracles with North American wildlife. Various disciplines of wildlife management are taught at colleges and universities throughout North America. Mexico has been a bit behind and is working hard to catch up, but American and Canadian wildlife biologists and managers comprise the world's largest communities in these professions and are highly respected around the globe.

Democracy of hunting. Among the sovereign nations of the world the only country known that guarantees hunting as a *right* in its constitution is the African nation of Botswana. In North America hunting is *not* a guaranteed right; it is a privilege. As such it is a privilege that can be taken away, and cessation of hunting privileges is often part of the penalty imposed on those who break game laws. However, since wildlife is a publicly held resource, the privilege to hunt or fish is extended to everyone within the confines of duly established laws. In some cases this is a simple matter of obtaining the proper qualifications (such as Hunter Safety certification), purchasing a license, and finding a place to hunt (which, in North America, includes millions of acres of public land). The harvest is regulated through length and timing of hunting seasons and of course harvest, or bag limits. In the case of fragile or more limited species, hunting is often further restricted by limited entry to certain areas or limited permits. In some cases these are first come, first served, but very common is allocation of permits by public drawing or lottery, a concept that is truly the "democracy of hunting" in action.

An Internet search of "North American Model" will turn up numerous sites and much information. The foregoing is the version preferred by most conservation organizations and is used by The Wildlife Society, which is a nonprofit scientific and educational organization dating back to 1937 (www. wildlife.org). The society is neither specifically pro-hunting nor specifically anti-hunting and is America's senior organization for wildlife professionals. However, there are some slight differences with other interpretations. For instance, another site that such a search will yield is the Arizona Game and Fish Department, whose slogan is "Managing Today for Wildlife Tomorrow." The very first part of their home page is about the North American model. They also have seven basic tenets, which they call "Arizona's 7 core concepts of conservation."

Although the wording and order are slightly different, six of their seven tenets are exactly the same as those preceding. This is the one that's different: The Arizona Game and Fish Department doesn't say "wildlife should be killed only for a legitimate purpose"; it appears that the department finds this to be implied under the due processes of law and science. Instead, one of its core concepts is very simple, extremely pragmatic, and very important: "Hunters and anglers fund conservation." Wow, that's a mouthful, and it is absolutely true. Their page goes on to ask—and answer—the question "What if hunting ends?"

Their answer starts with "Hunters and anglers actively support wildlife conservation through tangible actions such as buying licenses and paying taxes on hunting and fishing equipment." And, it goes on further to state that *"[t]here is no alternative funding system in place* [emphasis added] to replace the potential lost funds for conservation. If hunting ends, funding for wildlife conservation is in peril." Whether stated or not, this is part of the deal with North American wildlife management: Sports men and women foot the bill not only for the management and conservation of game species but also for the many nongame species they share their habitats with. This is the system that has developed, and especially in the current economic times there truly is no other funding alternative.

So, how did we get from a continent-wide wildlife disaster by about 1900 to the plenty we enjoy today? Well, it didn't start with today's sophisticated system of state and federal agencies, paid for by sports men and women and aided by private conservation groups, also funded by sports men and women. But it did start with a small group of hunters when Theodore Roosevelt and American anthropologist and naturalist George Bird Grinnell (1849–1938) formed the Boone and Crockett Club. Roosevelt had returned to New York after his Dakota ranch failed during the especially severe winter of 1885–1886. He was defeated in a bid for mayor, but much greater things lay ahead for him.

As a hunter there is no question but that Roosevelt participated in the excesses of his time, but he also understood that American wildlife was on its last legs. It was uncertain that the bison could survive and that most other Western species were in dire straits. The Boone and Crockett Club led the way back, working in the political arena to create parks and reserves to preserve what remained and working in the public arena to pioneer and foster "the responsible, ethical, and sustainable use of wildlife known as Fair Chase." To this day the Boone and Crockett Club remains a leader in conservation and in promoting the concept of fair chase that Roosevelt and Grinnell created. The cause was, of course, greatly aided by the presidency of one of its cofounders, Theodore Roosevelt, twenty-sixth president of the United States, from 1901–1909!

Since Roosevelt's day North American hunters have become one of the most self-regulating special-interest groups in the world. Seasons, bag limits, ever-escalating license fees, and more have been created by hunters for hunters and wildlife, and the success of these efforts can be seen in the amazing rebound of North America's wildlife resources. It didn't happen overnight, and with some species the process is still ongoing. Because protection came first, followed by science-based professional management, the majority of North America's native species have responded.

In 1937 the Federal Aid in Restoration of Wildlife was signed into law by President Franklin Roosevelt. Known as the Pittman-Robertson Act, this bill took an existing tax on firearms and ammunition and earmarked it for the Department of the Interior, which disburses the funds to the states for wildlife restoration and management. In recent years the tax has been added to archery equipment as well, and this continues to this day. Through this key piece of legislation, by 2010 American hunters contributed more than two billion dollars directly to wildlife conservation. Even this doesn't come close to completing the picture of hunters' contributions to North American wildlife. There are dozens of privately funded conservation organizations that contribute to wildlife conservation efforts. Some, like the Audubon Society and the Sierra Club, are openly neutral regarding hunting. Many organizations are supported primarily by hunters and often focus their efforts on certain species or types of wildlife, such as Ducks Unlimited, Foundation for North American Wild Sheep, Rocky Mountain Elk Foundation, and more. Other organizations funded by hunters are more general in their interests: Boone and Crockett Club, Dallas Safari Club, and Safari Club International. Here is a small piece of reality: The organizations that are openly anti-hunting contribute very little to our North American model. Hunters do, and that's the way our system works.

✦ Chapter Seven ✦

Game Management Around the World

Our North American model is unique, but to appreciate it properly, it's worth taking a look at how things are done elsewhere in the world. There is one constant: Around the globe, game management is funded primarily by hunters, but only rarely do hunters in other societies have the same opportunity and access as their American cousins.

Europe

In feudal times, hunting developed as the divine right of kings, parceled out in varying degrees to the lesser nobles. This absolute power of the monarchies started to erode quite early. The Magna Charta of 1215, between the King of England and his nobles, was perhaps the first step that led to the constitutional governments, including constitutional monarchies, which are most common in modern Europe. Over time elected and appointed officials took over duties once the province of the landed gentry. This included wildlife management and game laws, although the rights and prerogatives of European landowners often exceed those of their North American counterparts.

Depending on the country, there are similarities between the European style of wildlife management and the North American model, and there are also significant differences. Most European countries have a similar system of hunting seasons and requirements for licensing, but it is often far more difficult to obtain a European hunting license than it is in North America. Some countries, notably Germany, require extensive schooling, followed by practical and written exams. Shooting tests are also common. In Finland and Sweden, where moose are generally hunted in drives and thus are rarely standing still, the shooting test includes firing at a running moose target that moves along a track. In much of Europe hunters are also required to have a mandatory insurance policy.

Perhaps the biggest difference is that there is no intent for European hunting to be democratic, with equal opportunity for all. European hunting is about effective wildlife management and utilization of the resource, but in most countries it long has been established and accepted that a relatively small number of hunters will do the majority of the management and provide the lion's share of the funding.

Harvest goals are inviolate. Typically established by gamekeepers who monitor the herds throughout the year, the classic European system is to harvest by both sex and age class, trying to maintain a near-perfect balance not only within the herd but ensuring that the animals stay within the carrying capacity of their habitat. Trophy fees are common and often escalate with the size of the horns or antlers. These fees help pay the gamekeepers—who may be government employees on government reserves or employees of the landowner on private lands. Game meat is generally sold and has considerable value.

Personal bag limits as we know them are rare. In North America it depends on the harvest goal; in some states with an overpopulation of whitetails the bag limits are high: South Carolina has no limit on male deer, and Alabama has a buck a day limit—although the necessary harvest of female deer is closely monitored in both states. But in most states and provinces hunters are limited to just one or perhaps two male deer, with bonus antlerless tags as the population dictates. Europe is different. If the management goal in a given piece of land is twenty roebuck, it matters not at all who harvests them, provided the hunters are properly licensed and willing to pay the fees.

Harvest goals are set with care. Some European gamekeepers have formal education in the fields of wildlife management and biology, while others operate based on long experience. Management of wildlife is essentially science based, as with our (often) more formalized natural resource departments in North America, but the harvest goal is critical, and to achieve that harvest seasons are often much longer than we are accustomed to, sometimes six months and more. This works because there are far fewer hunters, and it's all about the harvest goal. Once that is achieved it doesn't matter whether the season is open or not; the hunting is finished.

The European continent is actually blessed with a wide range of game, with huntable populations of virtually all species. Most plentiful and widespread are probably the wild boar, European roebuck, and red deer, in that order. Although an altogether different genus and species—and much smaller—the roebuck is similar to our whitetail in habits and habitat, so it tends to be found around the edges of agriculture. The European red deer is closely related to our elk (though somewhat smaller) and, similarly, needs larger mountains and forests for habitat. Europeans love their deer, but the native wild boar is an extremely important big-game animal. Because they have a huge range, breed quickly, and do the same damage to crops and forests as our feral hog populations, seasons tend to be extremely long (sometimes year-round). In much of Europe the wild boar is the most accessible big game for the average hunter—but harvest goals are established and remain inviolate.

Much European hunting is based on a market economy, with high fees often required for large specimens, especially in the case of animals that are in high demand and limited supply, such as the various ibex (a large wild goat) and the European brown bear. This goes against our concept of the democracy of hunting, but European hunters, though limited in number, understand it and support their system. The European continent is composed of dozens of nations, each with its own hunting culture and unique set of traditions and ethics, so it is an admitted glittering generality to try to encapsulate the whole. The Baltic, Nordic, and Scandinavian countries have the highest *percentages* of hunters, although their numbers are smaller because these countries are much less populated than, say, France, Germany, and Spain—which also have very strong hunting communities.

Each nation has its own traditions as part of its hunting culture, but a common theme is respect for the animal and absolute adherence to the letter and spirit of its hunting laws. Because of their strong traditions, high ethics, and training they have performed, and a fairly common knowledge of the genuine role they play in wildlife management, European hunters, though small in numbers, are generally respected within their societies. There are issues regarding the question of hunting for certain animals, such as bears and wolves—as we have in North America—but most European societies accept the role of hunters and respect them for it. There was a popular bumper sticker in the Germanic regions that read *"Kein jagen, kein Wild,"* meaning literally "No hunting, no game." The European model is not the same as ours, but hunters support the vast majority of the continent's wildlife conservation efforts. And as is the case in North America, there are no known alternatives.

South America

Most countries in Latin America are about a century behind their North American neighbors in wildlife management. This is undoubtedly largely a result of political and economic instability throughout the nineteenth century and into the twentieth—and in some cases ongoing today—but whatever the root cause, most of South America's native wildlife is greatly depleted, and many species are in trouble. The international body, CITES, considers key species such as jaguar, ocelot, spectacled bear, pampas deer, marsh deer, and more to be endangered.

In actuality no species of large South American mammals has become extinct. Much good habitat remains, and most native species have pockets with viable populations. So there is hope, and in most cases the governments have enacted laws to protect wildlife. The largest problem is that there is a strong culture of subsistence hunting, and very limited traditions of ethical sport hunting. So in the back country, wildlife continues to dwindle, often hunted in the absence of law rather than its presence.

There are exceptions. Argentina has a strong hunting culture and is actually one of the world's largest "hunting destinations," welcoming more than twenty thousand visiting sports men and women annually. The majority come for the country's legendary bird hunting and are especially welcome because doves, pigeons, and even ducks and geese into the millions are a major plague in agricultural areas. Argentina also has carefully regulated hunting for a few native species—brocket deer, capybara, and peccary—and, additionally, has large free-ranging populations of several introduced species, including red deer, blackbuck antelope, fallow and axis deer, and the almost-universal feral hog.

Elsewhere in South America other countries similarly use bird hunting as a means of crop protection, and several countries are working hard to institute legal, regulated hunting both as an incentive for tourism and to place value on wildlife. Peru is now legally open to hunting of the small tropical white-tailed deer, with other opportunities under consideration. Brazil, a country that banned hunting altogether some years ago (with illegal hunting still common), has recently legalized hunting for nonnative species (feral hogs and water buffalo), and the government of Paraguay is working on instituting hunting laws. There is hope, but in South America much work lies ahead.

South Pacific

This is clearly not a "continent," but, as a region, it encompasses the continent of Australia, along with New Zealand and numerous islands. The big difference throughout this vast area is that, naturally, there were no populations of large mammals. In Australia, New Zealand, and certain larger islands, such as New Caledonia, early settlers introduced species from nearby Southeast Asia and Indonesia and from as far away as Europe and even North America. In some cases, as with feral hogs, goats, sheep, and water buffalo, this was done primarily to create alternative meat sources. In other cases it was done more or less as an experiment, to see whether seemingly empty but hospitable habitat could be occupied. Some experiments failed. In New Zealand experiments included Himalayan blue sheep and both mule deer and moose from North America. Apparently neither the blue sheep nor the mule deer established breeding populations, but the moose persisted for some years in the rugged Fjordland of New Zealand's South Island. Although there have been no confirmed sightings for fifty years, rumors still persist.

Most of these introductions were successful and, in some cases, much too successful. Today we know that the introduction of a nonnative animal may have serious effects on native fauna and flora, but in both New Zealand and Australia this realization struck long after the genie was out of the bottle. Water buffalo were introduced into Australia's Northern Territories in the 1830s and at one time existed in tens of thousands across Australia's Top End. Before motorized vehicles, Australia's vast sheep stations were serviced by donkey and camel caravans. When trucks came into use many of these animals were released into the seemingly limitless Outback. Today sheep ranchers share their grass with hundreds of thousands of feral donkeys and wild horses and in some areas thousands of feral camels.

In New Zealand numerous game species were introduced, and in favorable habitat and absence of predators many thrived, though some better than others. White-tailed deer from North America, for instance, were a gift during Theodore Roosevelt's presidency, but in more than a century have, they have established only two small populations. European red deer, on the other hand, expanded to nearly plague proportions, as did Himalayan tahr and European chamois in the high Alpine country.

Both New Zealand and Australia have strong hunting communities and generally share the same hunting ethics and culture of their European roots. So their game management has been a dichotomy of, on the one hand, conserving and preserving wildlife for recreational use and, on the other hand, elimination of invasive nonnatives because of habitat damage and, in the case of the water buffalo and banteng (another wild ox), transmission of the bovine diseases they carry to domestic stock.

The war against genuinely destructive nonnatives, such as feral hogs, goats, and donkeys, is ongoing and may never be won, but in most cases compromises have been reached. In much of Australia various introduced deer species are now managed as a resource, with seasons and licenses and opportunity much along the concept of the North American model. In the Northern Territories water buffalo were essentially eliminated but now roam freely in largely aboriginal-owned Arnhem Land and can be hunted with landowners' permission.

In New Zealand similar compromises have been reached. The New Zealand Deer Stalkers are a strong and politically active group that lobbies for conservation of introduced species, and New Zealand has a large outfitting industry with similar interests. The gross overpopulation of several introduced species was generally controlled decades ago, and now the government pursues a policy of elimination in some areas and management in others. Because of the extreme steepness of the Southern Alps and the lucrative venison market when red deer were overpopulated, the biggest challenge in New Zealand is the use of the helicopter. Both population control and, years ago, venison hunting for the market have largely been done by helicopter, a practice that clearly goes against any concept of ethical fair chase hunting. A challenge is that much of the Southern Alps are so steep and treacherous that access is possible only with technical climbing gear or by helicopter, so this is an issue both New Zealand hunters and their environmental agencies are attempting to solve.

Asia

As Earth's largest land mass Asia holds the world's greatest diversity in both habitats and animals, actually possessing greater species diversity than does Africa. It is almost impossible to quickly encapsulate such a huge area occupied by nations with widely differing cultures, but a primary character-istic is that throughout Asia there are very few sport hunting cultures. There are exceptions—Turkey has an active sport hunting community, as does Pakistan—but in general hunting in Asia has been (and is) subsistence based.

Unfortunately, there are vast stretches with little or no remaining wild-life. Part of the reason is unregulated hunting but part, too, is burgeoning human populations. India once had vast and diverse wildlife resources, but with a human population of 1.3 billion there is little room for wildlife, with remaining populations pushed into parks and reserves. Asia, however, is a very big place, and a lot of wild country offering excellent habitat remains.

A number of Asian countries have instituted sport hunting programs as a means of bringing in tourism, reducing poaching, placing value on wildlife, and funding management efforts. This is not the democracy of hunting op-portunity we have in North America, and, in a way, it is actually marketing of wildlife—but it works. The hunting countries of Asia retain viable wildlife populations that in many cases are increasing. In most of the Asian countries that do not have sport hunting programs poaching continues, and the wild-life continues to dwindle. Asian countries with successful programs include Azerbaijan, Armenia, Iran, Kyrgyzstan, Mongolia, Nepal, Pakistan, Russia, Tajikistan, and Turkey.

Africa

After North America, Africa probably holds the greatest wildlife reserves on the planet, and of course hosts a much greater diversity of species. Africa's biggest problem is its burgeoning human population, which, for wildlife, means ever-shrinking habitat. There are many African countries that have very little wildlife remaining—and indeed little room for recovery efforts. Other countries, Kenya being the most notable example, have set aside national parks where wildlife remains inviolate. Visitors to one of Kenya's great parks would have the impression that they are seeing a true paradise for wildlife. Indeed this would be true but only on a very limited scale; like many African countries, Kenya is crowded, and outside of her parks very little wildlife remains.

In fact, across the African continent the greatest remaining wildlife re-sources are found in the *hunting countries*. This seems a contradiction, but numerous African governments have learned the lessons mentioned above: that sport hunting places value on wildlife. In the African context this is much more than just a simple matter of license fees. Safaris bring local employment as well as all the other economic benefits of tourism. Photographic safaris do the same, but there is a difference: The photographic safari industry is generally viable only in well-maintained parks and especially in scenic areas. Hunting safaris are conducted in much more marginal areas that, in general, would not attract game-viewing tourism. The safari operators or outfitters typically fund the majority of the anti-poaching efforts within their hunting areas, and as an important by-product meat that is harvested is distributed, which further reduces the incentive to poach.

At this writing some twenty African countries have regulated sport-hunting programs. In most situations designated parks are not hunted, but hunting areas may be tribal lands, wildlife or forestry reserves, or private land. Africa's model of wildlife management varies from country to country but generally follows two paths: privatization and what might be termed "neo-colonialism"—and these may occur within the same country depending on who owns the land.

Privatization is simple: The person who owns the land also owns the wildlife and within broad governmental rules (such as protected species) is able to manage and harvest wildlife at his or her discretion. Although both coun-tries have tribal and government-owned lands that may or may not be hunted, privatization has been the salvation of wildlife in South Africa and Namibia. Thanks to an active hunting market—which places value on wildlife—both countries probably have more than ten times the wildlife that existed just thirty years ago. South Africa alone has some nine thousand registered game ranches. Some are hunted, some are used for photographic safaris, some are used for breeding purposes, and many are used for all three, but this incredible wealth of wildlife exists not just because it has value but because properly utilized wildlife has greater value than does livestock. South Africa and Namibia lie at the southern tip of the continent. Farther north private lands become less common, but there is also effective management and hunting on private lands in Botswana, Mozambique, Tanzania, Zambia, and Zimbabwe.

The other path is harder to understand. In the nineteenth century the European powers essentially carved up Africa into numerous colonial empires. Some colonial governments were more benign than others, but all utilized Africa's natural resources—including her wildlife—primarily for the enrichment of the mother country. In some countries effective wildlife management was pursued, in others not, but wildlife was often utilized as a source of revenue from tourism. Note, however, that the democracy of hunting as we know it was rarely practiced. The African tribes who had hunted for centuries were generally not allowed to hunt legally, so of course they became ever more adept at subsistence poaching.

When the colonial governments were replaced by African governments this status quo remained; wildlife was the province of the central government, and only rarely were the rural people allowed to resume legal hunting. Botswana is almost unique in the world in guaranteeing hunting as a right in its constitution, but Botswana is a large country, rich in wildlife, with a small human population. Rural Africans believe they have a right to their wildlife, and from their perspective they undoubtedly have a point. But today's human populations are simply too large to allow a democracy of hunting. This has existed de facto across much of Africa—with the result that entire countries are virtually devoid of wildlife.

In the hunting countries the central governments essentially market their wildlife much as the colonial powers did. The safari industries bring employment, conduct anti-poaching, and distribute meat, but this has not been enough to deter poaching either for subsistence or for the black market. Increasingly, both African governments and safari operators are sharing revenues directly with local villages, and many safari operators go several steps further by digging wells and building schools, providing further incentives to deter poaching. These are having positive effects in the hunting countries, but despite all management efforts Africa's fast-growing human population—and the resultant habitat loss—remains the greatest threat to Africa's wildlife.

Chapter Eight

Are *You* Interested? (Should *You* Be?)

In the eighteenth century most Americans seemed to believe that wildlife was limitless. In the nineteenth century it was widely held that wildlife needed to be removed for civilization to progress. It was almost too late when thinking changed, and in fact it was too late for the passenger pigeon, Merriam's elk, Audubon's bighorn, and several other animals. In the twentieth century we became stewards of the wild and came to realize that wildlife and humankind can coexist. Today we believe in science-based wildlife management.

Wildlife biology and related wildlife sciences are formal disciplines taught in colleges and universities across North America, and our system of wildlife management is the most advanced in the world. As we have seen, our North American model works extremely well for us, but not all of its tenets are precise fits for other countries and cultures. However, we do widely export the science. North American wildlife biologists and managers are constantly at work throughout the world, and prospective wildlife professionals from around the world come to North American schools for formal training.

As is the case with perhaps any other segment of society, there is a small minority of modern wildlife professionals who are opposed to hunting in any form. But in the main, modern wildlife science is based on sustainable utilization. Those who are genuine anti-hunters refuse to accept this and thus refuse to understand it, but our North American model of wildlife management is primarily based on and sustained by hunters. As the Arizona wildlife department pointed out, there is no plan for alternative funding.

In the United States our sixteen million licensed hunters (not a small group but only five percent of our population) pay the lion's share of all wildlife management costs. A related and larger group, America's gun owners, also contributes heavily through the Wildlife Restoration Act, which places an excise tax on firearms, ammunition, and archery equipment. Generally referred to as the Pittman-Robertson Act, after the bill's chief authors, these funds, earmarked specifically for wildlife management, are collected federally and distributed to the state wildlife agencies. Together, hunters (directly through hunting license sales and indirectly through the excise tax) and all who pursue any shooting sports, including archery, provide the funding for American wildlife management.

The hunters are the primary consumptive users of the wildlife they support, but they are certainly not the only Americans who enjoy today's bounty of wildlife. One supposes that it's possible for people to enjoy the outdoors and not enjoy wildlife—but it seems unlikely. So hikers, bikers, campers, birdwatchers, or anyone who admires a beautiful songbird or thrills to the sight of a deer slipping into the woods benefit from the American hunting community.

Unfortunately, as American society becomes increasingly urban, there are indeed many good people who, as Ruark, author of *Horn of the Hunter*, said, are "poisoned by city sidewalks and sentenced to a cement jungle"—and as a result take no personal pleasure and gain little or no benefit from our abundant wildlife. Americans who love the outdoors, whether hunters or not, may live in cement jungles, but most of them find ways to escape and find recreation amid nature. Such people, and this does include all hunters, are confused and perhaps horrified by the thought of an existence with no access to the great outdoors.

Humans, however, are adaptable creatures and manage very well in all of the world's climates and habitats, both natural and human made. We can get along just fine without almost anything save the bare essentials of life, especially if we don't know what we're missing. Just as there are many millions of Americans who enjoy the outdoors (many times more than America's hunters who fund that enjoyment), there are millions of Americans who have absolutely no exposure and thus have no concept of what they're missing.

As stated earlier, hunting is not for everyone. Our system of wildlife management is based upon a democracy of opportunity, in which all citizens in good standing can choose to participate or not, but that system is not based on any necessity for *all* Americans to be hunters. And despite the fact that hunters are the primary benefactors of both game and nongame species of wildlife, it is not necessary to be a hunter to enjoy America's wildlife. On the other hand, it is necessary to enjoy wildlife and the outdoors to be a hunter.

This alone suggests that hunting certainly isn't for everyone; many Americans are perfectly content as city dwellers and have no desire to escape their cement jungles, even briefly. For them our forefathers' promise of life, liberty, and pursuit of happiness doesn't include the outdoor experience.

That experience, however, is available for all. Most of the world's nations have set aside parks and reserves of one type or another both to conserve wildlife and allow outdoor recreation, but few societies have set aside the vast acreages of public lands that are available for North Americans to use. We have national, state, and provincial parks; national monuments; national forests; national grasslands; Bureau of Land Management (BLM) lands; wildlife refuges, and more. These various "set asides," like our wildlife resources, are held in public stewardship and carry different rules and levels of protection. Parks and monuments, for instance, are generally not hunted but are available for other forms of recreation. National forests and BLM lands—which comprise millions and millions of acres—are generally available for hunting as well as other forms of recreation. Hunting must be conducted in accordance with state and local game laws, and there are often rules, such as those pertaining to vehicular access, parking, and use of campgrounds; but in North America public land generally means just that, with the public having free access for recreational activities, which includes hunting where allowed.

So the opportunity to enjoy the outdoors is there, more available and at less cost than in most of the world's civilized societies. Does that stir any interest or at least a wee bit of curiosity? Maybe it does, maybe it doesn't. The hunter's horn doesn't sound for everyone, but outdoor activities are certainly not limited to hunting. The North American continent offers nature's wonders in every single region, in surprising proximity to our largest Eastern cities and not far from the urban sprawl of Los Angeles. People who love the outdoors find even a small patch of wild country both soothing and invigorating.

A stroll through the forest, a hike in the hills, a lazy afternoon on a riverbank, fishing pole in hand. Hunters, many nonhunters, and undoubtedly a few anti-hunters enjoy these activities equally. A hunter is always a hunter; it's part of his or her soul. A hunter is always looking through a lens slightly different from most people's, watching the ground for tracks and other signs, scanning the vegetation for a telltale hint of color or the texture of hair, or a glint of sun off antler or horn. But hunters are not actively hunting all the time, and most hunters are able to hunt only a small (but treasured) part of their time.

Understanding how close we came to losing all of our wildlife a century ago, every American should get at least a small thrill at the glimpse of a white-tailed deer or the overhead passage of a "V" formation of geese, but there is a leap from savoring the sight of a duck, pheasant, or deer to wanting to bring it to bag and serve it for dinner. Many people make that leap and at all stages in their lives, but many people don't. Some who might don't because they never have (or never create) the opportunity; others, regardless of opportunity, do not because the process doesn't interest them, and a few try it and reject it. The horn simply doesn't sound for them, and that's just fine, provided they don't stand in the way of those who hear it so clearly.

It's important to understand that hunting is not specifically about taking game. It's about being in the woods with that purpose in mind. This is a potential that all hunters savor. They spend countless hours planning and preparing their equipment, and the more optimistic among them have recipes in mind for the game they might harvest. However, all hunters also recognize that success is never assured. This is true the world over, but it's especially true in North America.

Our democracy of hunting, which is very much a good thing, puts a lot of hunters in the American woods during relatively short seasons. This is dictated by our opportunity to hunt in concert with the science of management, which sets a harvest goal to keep the game herds and their habitats healthy. But it doesn't mean that there's a buck, bear, or bull—or even a bird—for every single hunter on every single outing (or through the course of the season).

Hunters accept this willingly. It isn't the success that counts but the effort, being out there with hope and possibilities and accepting the outcome.

The taking of game is a *desired* outcome, but the probability varies greatly with time and place and also with random variables, such as weather, game movement, and activities of other hunters. Hunters deal with this gladly; much of the enjoyment is in the effort and also in the unknowable outcome. As hunters like to say, if success were a sure thing, it would no longer be hunting. But hunting does include the occasional killing of game, an event savored even more when it comes after significant effort and being skunked numerous times.

This is a complex combination of mind-set and emotions that hunters are hard put to explain, perhaps even more difficult than articulating exactly why they are hunters. The Spanish philosopher Ortega y Gassett, who was actually not a hunter himself, probably said it better and more clearly than any hunter ever has. In his *Reflections on Hunting*, Gassett said: "Hunters do not hunt in order to kill; they kill in order to have hunted."

Killing is not an everyday event in hunting, but it is an integral part of the process, as is the utilization of meat from the hunt, which humans have enjoyed since the birth of our species. It is generally not the hunting but rather the killing that some people find distasteful. Whether we accept it or not, death is a part of life, and hunting under modern wildlife management is truly the sacrificing of a few animals for the betterment of the herd, animals that can be spared or need to be taken because of limitations on food or habitat. This probably makes a great deal of sense to hunters and perhaps to some who are currently nonhunters, but some people will prefer to purchase their meat in cellophane wrapping or abstain from animal products altogether, and in our democratic society those options are OK too.

✢ CHAPTER NINE ✢

Keeping an Open Mind

Hunters are a passionate group but so are anti-hunters and the animal rights activists. As we have seen, the hunting community, though numbering well into the millions, isn't a large group compared to the overall population. However, they are generally supported by another allied group, America's gun owners, which the National Rifle Association believes to now number about eighty million. This is suddenly a very significant portion of America's population. The anti-gun activists are probably a larger group than the true anti-hunting zealots and the dedicated animal rights folks, but none of these groups, or all of them together, is actually as large as the hunters and gun owners whose activities they wish to curtail.

Their numbers are not precisely known. It is known, and somewhat to the dismay of the "antis," proven in survey after survey, that the majority of Americans support the concept of hunting for food and recreation and also support private ownership of firearms for legitimate purposes (which certainly includes hunting). Regardless of their actual numbers, the "antis" are dedicated and outspoken. Hunters are equally committed but often are not as outspoken, going about their business quietly and being quite bemused at the outrageous charges often laid against them.

Part of this is pure business. Modern humans, at least in Western society, have tremendous empathy for animals. Hunters love animals as much as anyone else—there's that seeming contradiction again—and as a group, hunters contribute tremendous amounts of money toward the well-being of wildlife. In 2011 alone, and totally exclusive of the monies spent on license fees and collected in excise taxes on their equipment, American hunters and anglers contributed over a billion dollars to private groups (nongovernmental organizations, or NGOs) dedicated to conserving wildlife. There are many such organizations at the local, state, federal, and international levels, but some good examples of pro-hunting conservation organizations are Ducks Unlimited, Dallas Safari Club, Pheasants Forever, Rocky Mountain Elk Foundation, Safari Club International, Wild Sheep Foundation, and the National Wild Turkey Federation. Later we will provide examples of the specific conservation activities of some of these groups, but for this discussion it's important to understand that hunters give generously for the betterment of the wildlife they love.

Other people also love wildlife and also give generously. And there are other organizations that are not pro-hunting (though not necessarily anti) that do very good work. Some that come to mind include the Audubon Society, The Nature Conservancy, the Sierra Club, and the World Wildlife Fund. And then there are groups that are genuinely and seriously anti-hunting, such as Friends of Animals, Humane Society of the United States (HSUS), and People for Ethical Treatment of Animals (PETA). A careful analysis of some of these groups suggests that they actually do relatively little for wildlife—but they are very good at raising money by playing on human emotions.

Often they get a bit careless with the truth, and one of their favorite tools is to create sympathy and raise money for "endangered species." This is in quotes because, if you check some of the literature and advertisements that are out there—or have been thrust upon you—it isn't uncommon to see a wide variety of species, from cougars to wolves to black bears and even white-tailed deer, called "endangered" in fund-raising literature.

"Endangered" is an accepted scientific status that means a species is in genuine danger of extinction unless major steps in preservation and conservation are taken. In the United States we have the Endangered Species Act (ESA), which places strong federal protection on species that wildlife scientists consider at risk of extinction. Internationally, the Convention on International Trade in Endangered Species (CITES), a treaty signed by the majority of the world's developed nations, performs the same function. Both ESA and CITES have their endangered species lists. This is not always perfect science; some species are listed on a cautionary basis because of lack of hard data, and some species that have recovered have been removed from the endangered lists.

There are, however, genuinely endangered species throughout the world that need and deserve extreme conservation measures. Worldwide, two well-known examples are the tiger and the giant panda. In the United States, the whooping crane was nearly gone. Incredible last-minute efforts staved off extinction, but the whooping crane is still very much endangered. The California condor is another good example. With only a handful of breeding pairs surviving in the wild, these big birds are *endangered*.

Genuine endangerment is extremely serious, obviously because extinction is forever and irreversible, but, less obviously, the effects of the loss of any given species on the other fauna and flora in the ecosystem are not always predictable. The misuse of the term "endangered" leads to two problems: First, it diverts attention (and funding) away from plants and animals that genuinely need help. Second, it creates the impression that the horrible hunters are willy-nilly killing endangered animals.

In general animals actually considered endangered are not hunted. This is absolutely true in the United States. Internationally, CITES has allowed some exemptions for limited sport hunting in specific situations whereby carefully regulated hunting has been demonstrated to be beneficial to the species. A good example is the black rhinoceros, seriously endangered across the African continent but recovered in South Africa and Namibia to the point where the international body deemed that a very small harvest of older, nonbreeding males would increase the value of the species and further aid in recovery. There are also a few seeming contradictions. CITES does not consider the polar bear endangered, but the United States has declared it so and placed it under the Endangered Species Act. This is a special situation worth further discussion later.

But here's the point: In the United States, species considered endangered are not hunted. This is generally true throughout the world, and it is true that ethical modern hunters do not hunt illegally and thus do not hunt endangered species.

Of course, in any big lie there are often small grains of truth. The mountain lion, or cougar, is often described as endangered. The actual population of mountain lions is not known—they are very secretive and hard to count—but it's safe to say that they roam somewhere in the tens of thousands, from southern Mexico, across the western United States, and north to Canada's treeline. It is also safe to say that the mountain lion is expanding its range, which suggests that its numbers are increasing. Nebraska now has a small breeding population for the first time in a century, and individual cougars have been positively identified far to the east of their known range. But here's the grain of truth: The "Florida panther," a smaller and isolated subspecies, is definitely threatened, if not genuinely endangered, and of course is fully protected.

The gray wolf, though still plentiful in western Canada and Alaska, was definitely endangered in the lower forty-eight states. Reintroduction efforts over the past quarter century have proven incredibly successful; some ranchers and wildlife managers would say *too* successful! There are now several thousand wolves, primarily in the Yellowstone region and the western Great Lakes—but wandering wolves have been seen throughout the Rocky Mountain West and as far south as Kansas. Recognizing the success of wolf recovery, at this writing, U.S. Fish and Wildlife is in the process of delisting the gray wolf within the United States, which means that the term "endangered" would no longer apply and management reverts to state wildlife agencies.

A hundred years ago, when white-tailed deer numbers were about a half million and dropping, it might have been appropriate to consider the whitetail to be threatened, but a population numbering into the hundreds of thousands can never be considered endangered. But there are tiny grains of truth. There are thirty-eight recognized subspecies, or races, of white-tailed deer, varying tremendously in body size and somewhat in color. Smallest of all is the little Florida Key whitetail. Primarily because of development and habitat loss they are endangered, fully protected, and of course not hunted.

Another little-known whitetail subspecies is the Columbian whitetail, a small race found in western Oregon, totally isolated from all other whitetails. The Columbian whitetail is found in heavily farmed and ranched valleys, and as towns sprang up it almost vanished. It was declared endangered in 1968 and came under the protection of the ESA. Protection, habitat improvement, and reintroductions—much of the last two by Oregon hunters—saved the day. The Columbian whitetail was delisted, with limited hunting resumed in 2005. Today the Columbian whitetail continues to increase and expand its range and is still hunted on a carefully managed basis.

In the case of the black bear being labeled endangered, it's difficult to find even the tiniest grain of truth. The grizzly bear is definitely endangered, and legally considered so, in the continental United States. But thanks to protection and good management the grizzly is recovering quickly in our Northern Rockies, and almost certainly certain populations will eventually be delisted. The black bear did indeed nearly vanish from much of its original range, especially in the East, but today has reoccupied much of that former range and in fact occurs in varying densities from the Atlantic to the Pacific, the primary exception being the Great Plains, which was never black bear habitat. Today it is protected where protection and recovery are still needed and hunted where a huntable surplus exists. The most recent state to reinstitute black bear hunting was New Jersey, where the population rebuilt to where problem bears were becoming, well, a problem.

One of the greatest myths in the wildlife world surrounds the plight of the endangered African elephant. Humans have always prized elephant ivory, with trade going back at least to Greek and Roman times. In the 1970s and 1980s, however, an unprecedented wave of commercial poaching swept Africa, primarily for the ivory carving industries in Asia. In a few short years elephants were literally erased from vast regions. The world woke up, almost too late, and in 1990 the International Ban on Ivory Trade went into effect. Ivory poaching has never been totally stopped, but the international ban, along with increased enforcement, greatly reduced the losses and the elephants began to rebuild.

Regrettably, in the recent down economy poaching of both elephant and rhino has escalated considerably, so a new crisis may lie ahead. But here's the point: The widespread commercial poaching of thirty years ago did not extend to all of Africa. At the lowest point, probably 1989, by most estimates there were still six hundred thousand wild elephants in Africa. The elephants were locally threatened in some areas and in a few major countries almost became extinct. As a species, however, the African elephant has never been endangered and in fact was thriving and continues to thrive in several countries, primarily in southern Africa. Although it sounds easy, counting elephants is almost impossible across the vastness of Africa. Today, low estimates place the wild elephant population to be around nine hundred thousand; high estimates range up to 1.3 million. Either way, the African elephant is not endangered and in fact in several countries is significantly overpopulated.

Zimbabwe, a small country with limited habitat, has about one hundred thousand elephants. Its neighbor to the west, Botswana, a larger country with a smaller human population, has the largest elephant population, about 150,000. And, yes, elephants are still hunted. From inception the ivory ban allowed exemption for "sport-hunted elephant trophies for personal use," subject to internationally regulated quotas, from countries able to prove to the international body that hunting was not detrimental. Today, there is legal, limited, and carefully regulated elephant hunting in a half dozen African countries. These countries hold the majority of the continent's elephant population, and it is primarily in these countries that elephant numbers are stable or increasing. This is because the hunting places value on elephants, funds management and anti-poaching efforts, and reduces human–elephant conflict. This last is fairly critical. American farmers often complain bitterly about whitetails eating their crops, but what about a hundred elephants in your cornfield? Elephants are extremely intelligent animals. A bit of hunting pressure reduces crop raiding, and the fees and local employment from safari hunting make up for some of the losses.

Here's what's important: People have strong feelings on the subject of hunting, often based on emotions but not always on facts. Educators are as human as anyone else. Some have agendas, whether political, sociological, environmental, or anti-gun or anti-hunting. Many, however, are non-hunters just like the majority of the American population. They are just as prone as any of us to place trust in the media. After all, if it's printed or shown on TV it must be true, right? Not necessarily. There are many myths and misconceptions on hunting, ecology, wildlife management, environmental issues, that knotty question about firearms ownership, and many other things that are accepted as gospel and passed along as gospel, whether knowingly or unknowingly.

Never hesitate to question! There are, of course, times to question publicly and times when it's wiser to ask the questions to yourself and then seek the true answer. This book is intended to provide concepts, ideas, and facts on the subjects of hunting, wildlife management, and firearms ownership. We as hunters believe the information herein to be true, and it certainly is to the best of our ability. But we are hunters, so don't hesitate to do your own research. The Internet, school and public libraries, and so many other sources are crammed with information on these subjects. As with all sensitive, emotion-charged issues, reliability varies. So keep an open mind, do your own digging, and come to your own conclusions. In any rational and objective analysis, sport hunting and modern hunters come off pretty well.

✦ Chapter Ten ✦

Notes on First Hunts

No matter at what age it takes place, a person's first hunt is a major milestone, an event likely to be remembered for the rest of his or her life. It may or may not be a life-changing event. Some people have that gene coursing through their bodies, and they know for years that this is something they wish to do. Others may be mildly curious or perhaps pushed into the experience by a family member or friend. Chances are the experience will be pleasant, but if the gene isn't there or the person isn't ready to hear the horn, then it won't be a mind-altering event. On the other hand, that innate desire to be a hunter may simply be latent, waiting to surface. That first hunt could well awaken the sleeping giant.

Traditionally, most hunters were brought into the fraternity by their fathers or grandfathers, or perhaps an uncle. Traditionally, too, in hunting families male children were often given this chance, and female children were often denied it. As we have seen, this is changing. Daughters are, properly, being given equal opportunity to make hunting part of their lives or simply to have the experience and thus gain a lifelong and invaluable understanding of what it's all about. But mothers are also hunters and often assume the responsibility of bringing their sons into the sport.

A recent Internet post spoke volumes about the changing sociology of hunting. Josh, a young teenager, wrote, "My mom is taking me pig hunting in Louisiana. We have a 6.8 mm available. Do you think that rifle will be adequate?"

The obvious is that Josh's mother (good for her!) is taking her son hunting. This scenario would have been rare a generation ago but is becoming increasingly common today. But there's more. For the past forty years the white-tailed deer has been the most available game animal for the largest number of American hunters. This has not changed, but our rapidly expanding feral hog populations are creating new hunting opportunities and are among the few factors that are doing this. Feral hogs are prolific and destructive and are increasing rapidly in both numbers and range. Although some jurisdictions consider them big game animals, in most states they receive minimal legal protection. Seasons are long (or wide open), and the meat is good. Farmers dislike them because of their rooting behavior and depredation to crops, so many landowners who may not allow access for deer hunting welcome hog hunters. Once confined to a very few specific areas, feral hog populations are on the move. The animals are now widely distributed through the South and up and down the West Coast, and although a bit spottier in the North, they are rapidly working their way toward the middle.

Feral hogs are changing the face of American hunting, and as game animals they offer advantages for youngsters and beginning hunters: They are generally not considered cute and cuddly and elicit minimal sympathy, and in most situations any hog is legal game. This greatly increases chances for success, and pork from a medium-sized sow is considerably better than that from a smelly old boar.

Then there's the cartridge Josh was asking about, which also speaks volumes. Remington designed the 6.8 mm special purpose cartridge (SPC) as a military round. It was sized to fit the military M16 or civilian AR15 action, with a .277-caliber bullet, which produces considerably more energy than the 5.56 mm NATO (.223 Remington) round. Although a few special operations units use it, the cartridge hasn't found widespread favor with the military. It has, however, become popular with civilian shooters and hunters who wish to hunt with their ARs. The 6.8 mm SPC was designed specifically for the AR action and has been chambered in very few other sporting firearms. So it's a reasonably safe assumption that the rifle Josh has available to use is a semiautomatic sporting rifle on the Armalite-designed AR15 action. We will touch on the modern semiautomatic sporting rifle in a later chapter, but this type of firearm is currently the hottest seller in the American market and is manufactured by more than ninety companies, small and large. We don't know whether it's his mom's, his dad's, or his own rifle, but his question says much about sporting arms in use in America. And, yes, his 6.8 mm SPC is plenty adequate for hogs.

We don't know whether Josh's planned hog hunt was successful. We hope it was, but like all hunting, not every beginner's first hunt is going to be successful, so perhaps it's even more important to hope that he enjoyed the experience. We also don't know exactly where he might be in terms of training, preparation, and experience. Generally speaking, one doesn't just wake up some morning, decide to be a hunter, and go hunting. There is a necessary process involved, and although only a parent or someone nearly as close can determine when a young person is ready, even beginning adults have steps they should go through.

Just perhaps, before one actually hunts, it's a good idea to participate as an observer. This is how most hunters start who are brought into the sport in the traditional way, generation to generation. This can happen at a very young age. Many hunting parents take toddlers afield with them, and many more allow young children to go along and enjoy the hunt before they're old enough to use firearms or bows. This is beneficial because it gives even young children a good sense of what's going on and, over time, a sense of whether they wish to continue when they're old enough. It's also not a bad idea for adults. Most people, female or male, who "marry into" hunting, for instance, don't immediately become hunters. Instead they go along to observe and learn. At some point some decide to participate, and others don't. This type of familiarization doesn't require wedding vows with a hunting spouse. Older children—teenagers—and adults who are not part of a hunting family but have even the mildest interest or curiosity can find (or make) friends who hunt and go along to see what it's all about.

Realistically, children born into hunting families don't always have choices, at least not at young ages. Regardless of what it happens to be, parents who are avid and dedicated to any hobby or pastime are likely to expose their children to it, and while choosing to hunt is a very personal decision, it's really up to the parents to make those initial exposures enjoyable. This book is intended primarily for younger people—not their parents—but there's a caution here worth mentioning. Hunting is not especially easy for young children. It may or may not require a great deal of physical exertion, but it does require patience and the ability to focus and remain quiet. Some people are just naturally better at these things than others, and perhaps people get better as they get older. But new hunters, and especially younger children, need to be treated gently. That all-important memory of a first hunting experience will not be pleasant if it's characterized by being cold, hungry, bored, and constantly being scolded for fidgeting and making noise.

It's natural for younger children to want to do what their parents do, and it's equally natural for their parents to want to take them along. But both physical and mental capabilities must be taken into account lest the child be turned off rather than turned on to hunting. Teenagers and adults who have had no exposure to hunting but are curious may have to work harder to gain the opportunity but have full capability to embrace it. Just going along on short, local hunts with friends or family is a fine way to enjoy the outdoors and gain a sense of whether this hunting thing is of interest.

If you find it's something you want to do, then more work lies ahead. Hunting is not really a complex endeavor, but it takes more steps than grabbing a rifle or bow and heading into the woods. Regulations vary considerably, but most states and provinces today require completing a hunter safety course before a hunting license can be purchased. Curricula also vary, but this training is good and essential. Most hunter safety courses provide a great deal of information on hunting in general and local conditions, as well as the obvious on safety and game regulations. In fact, hunter safety training is such good stuff that it's recommended even for people who have not yet made a firm decision to actually hunt.

Although it's not clear whether the chicken or the egg should come first, along with mandatory hunter safety certification, prospective hunters must attain not just proficiency but absolute safe handling with whatever equipment (gun or bow) that they intend to hunt with. This is often a lot easier for kids from hunting families. A normal progression would be a BB gun at a fairly young age and, after a broken window or two (and resulting punishments), a few years later a .22 or small shotgun and lots of practice under close supervision. By the time the child is actually old enough and ready to hunt, the expertise and safe-handling procedures are already in place.

It is more difficult to come in cold, but the ability to use hunting arms safely and proficiently is an absolute prerequisite to hunting. The next chapter will offer some suggestions and resources for getting started, but there are no shortcuts here. All hunters miss occasionally and not all shots that hit are always perfect, but ethical hunting requires enough proficiency to ensure a high probability of a well-placed shot and safety is always paramount.

Once these qualifications are met and the new hunter is licensed (if required), then he or she is ready to go afield. Ideally, a new hunter should have a mentor of some type—parent, uncle, spouse, friend—who is more experienced and can further the education process on hunting techniques and game habits and habitats. But for hunters of all ages, and especially new hunters, the buddy system is best for both safety and success.

So let's talk about success. It would be a wonderful thing if every hunter's first hunt was successful, but that's not the real world. As said before (and will be said again), the white-tailed deer is America's most widespread and plentiful animal, so for many hunters its pursuit will be their first hunting experience. America's thirty-six million whitetails are pursued by about ten million hunters, so there are enough deer for everyone; but not every whitetail hunter will bag a deer. The whitetail deer has been well educated by generations of hunters, and no animal on Earth is more wary. Nationwide, hunter success on whitetailed deer rarely exceeds forty percent. If we're talking about bucks, it's lower, and if we're talking about *mature* bucks, much lower still, and in general it's lower on public land.

Realistically, then, not every hunter can expect to harvest a deer every year. Killing game is part of hunting, but even first-time hunters must understand that taking game doesn't happen on every hunt and that, although the possibility is there, in many cases, it's remote enough that it can't be the only reason to be in the field. Savor the sunrise and sunset, and although a certain species is probably the target, observe and enjoy all of nature—songbirds, small animals, even insects. The natural world is wonderful, and as a hunter you are part of it—but if you're there just for the killing you're on the wrong track.

That said, harvesting game is part of the experience, and it's beneficial for new hunters to have that experience as early in their hunting careers as possible. So, although beginner's luck really is a powerful tool, don't set your sights on the biggest buck in the woods. Today, state wildlife agencies are working hard to encourage young hunters, with special youth seasons and youth hunts on designated state lands. These are great opportunities for young hunters to take advantage of.

Antlerless harvests are allowed in some areas because the deer herd is approaching or exceeding the carrying capacity of the habitat and a harvest of does is necessary to keep the herd at the desired level. Take advantage of this opportunity; plenty of years lie ahead to look for that big buck, and a nice, fat doe yields the tastiest of venison.

Spencer's dad was not a deer hunter, but Spencer was one of those young-sters who had long known he wanted to hunt and that he wanted to hunt deer. He did his hunter safety course, and his dad taught him to shoot. They secured permission to hunt on a friend's farm, and they built a stand overlooking major trails along an oak ridge. Spencer was fortunate to live in an area with lots of deer and to have a dad who understood how important it was to him. He was eleven when he shot his first deer, a fine doe, from that stand. In seasons that followed, the same stand yielded several more deer, including a couple of nice bucks. Now in his midteens, Spencer is an accomplished deer hunter, and his dad, who always hunts with him, has never shot a deer.

Although deer hunting is America's single most popular hunting pursuit, it is certainly not the only option. Most beginning hunters probably start with small game, rabbits and squirrels; many start with upland game and waterfowl. And, as mentioned earlier, the proliferation of wild hogs is creating excellent opportunities for new hunters. Caroline was twelve when she obtained her hunter safety certificate, and she had spent time on the range learning to shoot with her dad. But she had never shown any real interest in hunting until she was sixteen, when, to her dad's surprise, she asked if she could shoot a wild hog.

It was spring, but in their area feral hogs are a year-round season. So they dusted off her hunter safety card and did some refresher training at the range. One afternoon her dad picked her up from cheerleading practice, and they drove out to a friend's ranch and set up above a waterhole. It was nearly dusk when a nice boar stepped out of the woods, and Caroline dropped it with a perfect shot. Until that moment she wasn't sure whether she wanted to hunt, but she was curious about it. That afternoon she became a hunter.

CHAPTER ELEVEN

If You Want to Hunt . . .

Children of hunters, as well as spouses or girlfriends and boyfriends who join a hunting family, definitely have a leg up. But that's true of a lot of complex hobbies and endeavors, from playing chess to barrel racing. America truly is the land of opportunity, and like most everything else hunting is a sport that "unconnected" people can get involved in if they want to badly enough; it just takes a bit more effort if no one in your close circle of family and friends happens to be a hunter.

Hunting is *not* a team sport. Although it's wonderful to share the outdoors with people you love, and, as stated earlier, the buddy system is always best for safety, hunting is actually a solitary endeavor. A buddy, mentor, or guide may assist you in finding game—and hopefully will help you get it out of the woods! But the decision to shoot or release the arrow is altogether up to you, as is the proper aiming of your projectile. But when it comes to getting involved in hunting, you do have a team. It's a very large team composed of sixteen million American hunters.

While it's true that some of them do indeed prefer to hunt alone, it's also true that all American hunters are keenly aware of the constant necessity to recruit new hunters into their ranks to preserve the hunting culture for the future. It is also true that most hunters are eager to share the experience they love so much. So most sports men and women are delighted to welcome new hunters into their ranks. For younger people there are indeed issues with parental consent and liability, but these can usually be overcome. The biggest challenge for people who are interested in the outdoors but who come from families who are not is finding people who are.

This is not actually as difficult as it sounds; it's simply a matter of finding a team and joining it. As said earlier, it isn't a bad idea to get an introduction to the outdoors before trying to jump straight into hunting. The Scouting movement, for both girls and boys, is neither pro-hunting nor anti but very much in favor of the outdoor experience, and Scouting is nationwide, with troops in every major city in America. A Scout campout is not a hunt, but it's a wonderful introduction to the outdoors where woodcraft and survival skills (along with teamwork and leadership) can be learned that will remain valuable for a lifetime. In more rural communities, 4H programs are also winners. They also are not specifically pro-hunting, but 4H-ers believe in the outdoors and the environment.

It also follows naturally that, while not all outdoorspeople are hunters, all hunters are outdoorspeople, so these are groups in which young people are very likely to find both leaders and peers who are hunters. These youth programs take no political stance regarding either hunting or firearms, but summer camps often include both archery and shooting as available activities. There are many hunters today who learned their shooting skills at a Boy Scout camp.

Another good option for prospective hunters of all ages—or even people who are mildly curious—is to take their state's hunter safety course. Aside from being invaluable training and, usually, a prerequisite for licensing, a hunter safety course is a wonderful way to make friends with other hunters. The websites of most wildlife agencies will list scheduled courses, but here's an even better way: Go to a sporting goods store or gunshop in your neighborhood and ask!

Gunshops are major focal points for hunters and shooters. Clearly they're in business to be in business, so you can't be a pest when the salespeople are busy with customers. But, just as clearly, it's in their best interests to make new customers! Most gunshops and firearms departments in chain stores will post dates and times for hunter safety courses. Also, you can put in the bank that most people who work those counters are shooters and probably hunters, and so long as business isn't crazy they will willingly share information. Many current hunters who did not come from hunting families tell about getting their start in small gunshops, dreaming dreams and making friends.

There are also some larger teams you can get involved in. Largest of all is the National Rifle Association. Perhaps best known as America's foremost group in protecting Americans' rights to own firearms under the Second Amendment to our Constitution, the NRA is a lot more than that. They are the primary body in managing rifle and pistol competitions in the United States, but, more to the point for this discussion, they have affiliated rifle and pistol associations in most states, and they also have active youth programs across the country, with a network of ninety-seven thousand qualified instructors and range safety officers. One of their successful programs includes Eddie Eagle, a cartoon-based safety message that teaches youngsters, upon finding an unsecured firearm, to "Stop! Don't touch. Leave the area. Tell an adult." You can visit the NRA and surf their programs and contacts at www.nra.org.

Safari Club International is probably the largest single hunting organization. Active in both lobbying for hunters in the political arena and conservation efforts, their motto is "first for hunters," and on both a national and international level they truly are. However, Safari Club International (SCI) is organized into several hundred local chapters. There are Safari Club chapters throughout North America and in most cities in the United States. For beginning hunters the name "Safari Club" may sound intimidating, but its membership is just dedicated hunters with all levels of experience. Many Safari Club chapters have active youth programs, and every one of them welcomes people of all ages who are interested in learning about hunting. Most chapters have regular monthly gatherings, and guests are welcome. For information on SCI's programs and to find a chapter in your area, check its website at www.safariclub.org.

Nationwide there are innumerable regional, state, and local hunting organizations, some affiliated nationally. It isn't difficult to find hunters, and if you find hunters you will find hunters who will welcome you. Learning to shoot, which is clearly a prerequisite to actually hunting, is a slightly different issue. Hunters' groups have programs that will help, and so will many individual hunters. As mentioned earlier, most Scouting camps have shooting and archery programs, and the NRA offers a variety of training programs. At the grassroots level, there are also hundreds of public shooting ranges, including indoor ranges, in all major cities. Because the backstop requirement is simpler and environmentally easier (no fumes to vent and no lead pollution to contain), there are also lots of archery ranges, including indoor ranges in many archery tackle shops and sporting goods stores. All offer training programs, and all are in the business of making new shooters.

Commercial training options are not free but also are not particularly expensive. Indoor ranges often rent firearms, and of course they're happy to sell ammunition in small quantities, so learning to shoot doesn't necessarily require any major expenditure in equipment. Even a bit of formal training with a good instructor is very helpful in getting started shooting. Bad habits are avoided, and proper form and technique can be learned, and professional instructors are really good at drumming basic safety procedures into new shooters. Especially for adults with no history in the shooting sports, a few sessions with a professional coach can really jump-start their skill level.

That said, most people start informally by going to a range—or any safe place to shoot—with a family member or friend. That's OK, too. Generations of youngsters have learned archery with small bows and rubber cup–tipped arrows, and these skills actually provide a good background for moving up to serious target and hunting bows. The good old BB gun, too, provides an inexpensive basis for moving up to more powerful guns. Even a BB gun is dangerous, so safe handling must be stressed. The primary training tool for all shooters of all ages, however, is the .22 Rimfire. It is the most popular cartridge in the world, with annual cartridge sales into the billions (yes, billions!). It is small, minimal in report and recoil, and inexpensive to shoot but also lethal; so however a new shooter starts and by whomever he or she is coached, the first and most important lessons must always be firearms safety. Regardless of age, a new shooter unfamiliar with firearms should be supervised by an experienced shooter. At first almost everyone needs to be reminded of basics such as always assume any firearm is loaded, mind the safety catch, and keep the barrel pointed in a safe direction.

In this modern world there's another great training tool: video simulations and video games. There is a genuine and perhaps legitimate concern that the amazingly vivid screen images desensitize people to violence, so it's important to remember that video games aren't real but that real guns firing real bullets do real damage. However, the sight alignment skills are transferable to the real thing, and some games are accurate enough that even the manipulation of a firearm's action can become familiar.

For instance, Luke, a midteenager, had never even seen a real AR15 rifle, but when his cousin took him to the range he knew from video games exactly how to insert the magazine, load the chamber, manipulate the safety, and align the sights. Both military and law enforcement use computer simulations for training, and there are some excellent hunting video games available. Nothing takes the place of actual range time, though, but when viewed as training tools video games offer valuable low-cost options that can increase the speed at which actual shooting skills can be acquired. The primary caution is that it is impossible for a simulation to emphasize firearms safety to the degree that is necessary at the range or in the field. So, although these games that so many young people play today do offer useful training, it's important not to carry away the wrong lessons. Real guns are not toys!

CHAPTER TWELVE

Hunters: Self-Limiting and Giving Back

According to the most recent surveys, the actual number of American hunters increased by nearly nine percent during the first decade of the new millennium. It is understood that the majority of people today are not hunters, and it is also understood that in our increasingly urban society hunters are not growing as a percentage of the population. However, most people—hunters, non-hunters, and even the most rabid anti-hunters—have at least some appreciation for wildlife. For many city dwellers this is purely an armchair interest best enjoyed on television, but it's a reasonable assumption that most people want wildlife to exist, persist, and procreate in our forests and fields.

If that premise is accepted, then accept further that, while the majority of Americans have some appreciation for wildlife, most who are not directly involved have little knowledge of how wildlife is managed and the role both hunters and hunting play in that management. In that context and often bombarded by anti-hunting propaganda, it's pretty easy to understand why some non-hunters think it's terrible for hunters to go around shooting America's vanishing wildlife!

As we have already seen, here in North America this is simply not true. The hunting that is done is based on the science of sustainable yield, managing the animals in relation to the habitat they have available. Although the models differ, this is also true throughout Western civilization. There is no group that has done as much for wildlife as hunters. This must be taken into account in any rational discussion of the question of hunting. In fact, it comes down to a very simple question that hunters should ask non-hunters and non-hunters should ask anti-hunters: If not hunters, then who?

In North America, and indeed throughout the civilized world, *hunters* are the ones who have created game laws—not non-hunters and not anti-hunters. *Hunters* are the people who have instituted license fees that, for the public good (and not just for their own benefit) pay for wildlife management. *Hunters* are the people who have limited their own activities by advocating for, assisting lawmakers draft, and helping to enforce our complex system of seasons, bag limits, and legal hunting methodology. Hunters are thus the most self-limiting group on Earth, not only willing to accept but in most cases recommend laws that further limit their own hunting activities.

We hunters do this because we have seen that our system works, and we genuinely understand that, especially here in North America, we have brought our wildlife from rags to riches. The real conservation movement in North America began with the Boone and Crockett Club in 1887. As an organization Boone and Crockett has always been small in membership, but remains an influential force in conservation and in promoting the ethics of "fair chase" hunting, a term and concept coined by B&C. In 1887 it already seemed almost too late to save the tattered remnants of North American wildlife, but fortunately game populations are resilient, and, equally fortunately, the crisis was recognized and in most cases the carnage was stopped before it was too late.

The cure was simple, though not so easily executed, and it was essentially a two-step process. First, hunters had to limit their activities. This process actually started in the earliest years of the Colonies, with local ordinances passed not exactly to *conserve wildlife* but to perpetuate what was then a source of revenue for some and a critical food source for many. Clear back in 1646 whitetail deer hunting was closed in New York from May 1 to November 1, with a fine imposed for out-of-season hunting. Connecticut and Massachusetts also established deer hunting seasons before 1700 (which means that year-round hunting was no longer allowed). In 1739 the General Court of Massachusetts beefed up the enforcement, directing each town to appoint two "deer reeves"—what we would call game wardens. The fine for taking a deer out of season was ten pounds, a huge sum in that day, with half to the town and half to the warden or reeve as his payment for execution of his duty.

These steps were obviously taken to conserve what was probably already a dwindling resource in these smaller and most heavily populated colonies. According to The Wildlife Society, by the time of the American Revolution many towns had already abandoned the system of deer reeves because there were too few deer left to protect. These early efforts showed a need to preserve an important resource and established the mechanism—law—to provide that protection. As we have seen, this remains one of the seven tenets of our North American model of wildlife conservation.

Over time, as that model of wildlife conservation developed and professional, science-based management took hold, hunters continued to accept more limitations, willingly accepting shortened seasons and closures, shrinking bag limits, and an ever-increasing host of restrictions so that wildlife might first recover and then persist for future generations. The Adirondack Deer Law, passed by the New York State Assembly in 1897 at the urging of both the New York Sportsmen's Club and Boone and Crockett, was a signal piece of legislation that outlawed spotlighting deer at night and shooting deer after using hounds to drive them into deep water. An important underlying principle of this law, one of the very first of its kind, was that it outlawed unsportsmanlike behavior rather than simply restrict the harvest.

This concept of "sportsmanship," what the Boone and Crockett Club came to define as "fair chase," is extremely important to the concept of modern hunting and perhaps difficult for non-hunters to understand. It isn't just a matter of killing an animal; to a hunter it matters greatly *how* that animal is harvested: The hunting must be in accordance with all existing laws, and the animal must have full opportunity to use its natural instincts and capabilities to escape.

Today North American hunters are legally compelled to adhere to a fairly complex array of regulations that establish legal hunting hours, equipment that may be used, and hunting methods. These often vary by state and season. For example, our most common hunting hours are a half hour before sunrise to a half hour after sunset, but some states mandate sunrise and sunset. In more specialized circumstances, some states require wild turkey hunters to be out of the woods at noon, while for many years South Dakota hunters were not allowed to harvest pheasants *before noon*. Many states have caliber or cartridge restrictions for deer, while many jurisdictions allow (primarily for safety reasons) only shotguns and muzzleloaders during firearms seasons—and there are often entirely different sets of regulations for archery and muzzleloader seasons.

Today, with our science-based management, each state has different management goals. Some states must chronically contend with overpopulation of deer, which leads to increased road hazard, damage to flora, escalating crop depredation, and risk of disease. Other states, often in the West (where winter kill and drought are periodic concerns), have a more fragile situation whereby the harvest must be carefully regulated. Seasons and bag limits are primary management tools, but allowable methods also come into play. Many Southern, some Midwestern and a few Northern jurisdictions, for instance, usually where a larger harvest is desirable, allow baiting for deer, a method that is totally illegal in much of North America and thus is a hotly debated issue among hunters and game managers alike.

Not all hunters agree with all decisions made by their wildlife managers and game commissions. But today's sports men and women obey the game laws—*all* the game laws, wherever they hunt. Every barrel has its bad apples, but there is another word for the few who don't follow the game laws. We call them poachers, and no ethical hunter abides them. Most state game departments have hotlines whereby observed or suspected unlawful hunting can be called in, and in fact a large percentage of poaching arrests come from tips from lawful hunters. Well, they should, because a poacher is stealing wildlife from hunters and non-hunters alike and also gives lawful and ethical hunters a black eye.

The second essential component in North America's amazing wildlife recovery was that hunters had to start giving back. Few groups on Earth have shown as much forbearance or been as generous as hunters. The science-based wildlife management that we enjoy on this continent is funded almost entirely by hunters and fisher men and women. License fees are a major component. They continue to increase, but that's only one element. Over the years more and more extras have been added. Since its inception in 1934 the federal duck stamp program has raised $750 million for wetland conservation. Funds from this program alone have protected six million acres of wetland habitat, an area about the size of Vermont, with benefit for all species that utilize these habitats. States have followed with special-purpose upland game stamps, trout stamps, big-game stamps, conservation stamps, and more.

Hunters aren't much different from most other groups in our society: They aren't really happy unless they have something to complain about. So, of course, hunters complain about the rising costs and the added complexity of all those extra stamps and tags to enjoy their pastime. The federal duck stamp, required to hunt migratory species, now costs fifteen dollars, but, despite the complaining, hunters do as they do with all the required licenses and tags: They reach into their wallets and pay the freight.

Then there's the previously mentioned Wildlife Restoration Act, commonly called Pittman-Robertson after its primary sponsors, a federal excise tax on firearms and ammunition and, later, archery equipment, earmarked by law for the benefit of wildlife. Since 1939 Pittman-Robertson funding has generated $7.2 billion for conservation. This, obviously being a good idea, was later followed by the Sport Fish Restoration program, a similar excise tax on fishing equipment. Since 1952 this tax has yielded $7.3 billion for fishery improvement. In 2012 alone these two revenue streams yielded $371.3 million (Wildlife Restoration) and $350 million (Sport Fish Restoration) for conservation. As all humans are wont to do, they complain bitterly about the rising costs of their equipment, but no one has ever heard a single whine about the excise tax raising the price—it's just part of the deal.

✢ Chapter Thirteen ✢

Conservation Organizations

American hunters (and anglers) fund conservation through a complex and diverse system of licenses; permits; and extras, such as stamps. Some are voluntary, and some are required to hunt certain species or classes of game, such as waterfowl and upland birds. Hunters who wish to take part in hunting seasons for these specific birds or mammals must pay the necessary fees, but here's a funny thing about hunters: Many pay voluntarily. Annual sales of the federal duck stamp, for instance, considerably exceed the number of hunters who actually participate in waterfowl seasons. It is no doubt true that a lot of hunters purchase a full range of hunting and fishing licenses, sort of like an annual ritual, and have the best intentions of trying to use all of them. But many hunters purchase licenses and stamps with no intent to actually use them. Rather, this is just a small way of helping out or giving back.

A hunter safety certificate is often required to buy a hunting license, so even the best-intentioned non-hunter may not be able to contribute in that fashion. But there are no such prerequisites for purchasing federal duck stamps and the various state conservation stamps, so non-hunters and even anti-hunters can use those outlets to contribute directly to wildlife (although few besides hunters actually do). *All* gun owners, many of whom don't actually hunt, contribute to wildlife through the Pittman-Robertson excise tax.

Collectively, millions and millions of dollars flow to the state wildlife agencies annually, but even this is not enough.

The Boone and Crockett Club was America's first conservation organization, started by hunters and still a hunters' organization. Members of Boone and Crockett essentially saved the American bison from extirpation and were responsible for the creation of some of America's first national parks in full knowledge that these lands would not be available for hunting. But that was more than one hundred twenty-five years ago, and over time dozens of local, regional, and national conservation organizations have sprung up and have been supported by hunters. In 2011 alone hunters and fisher men and women contributed more than 1.1 billion dollars to private conservation organizations.

They run the gamut, from species-specific groups, such as Ducks Unlimited, Mule Deer Foundation, National Wild Turkey Federation, Rocky Mountain Elk Foundation, and Wild Sheep Foundation, to broad-based organizations, such as Safari Club International and Dallas Safari Club. It should be noted, however, that even the most specialized groups do good for much more than just their target species. A waterhole project by California's chapter of the Wild Sheep Foundation may enhance desert bighorn lamb survival on a specific desert mountain, but all other species present will benefit; a piece of wetland restored by Ducks Unlimited benefits all species that occupy the habitat, game and non-game alike. Winter elk range spared from development by the Elk Foundation may also be the salvation of the local pronghorns and mule deer.

As with purchasing conservation stamps, it is not necessary to be a hunter to support these organizations, and in fact many characterize themselves first as conservation organizations, not as hunting groups. But if you visit their conventions and fund-raisers you will quickly see that hunters are the primary supporters, contributors, and workers. It would be impossible to detail all the accomplishments of all the groups, but here are a few examples of what hunters and their dollars have accomplished and are accomplishing.

This book focuses primarily on big game rather than on the wonderful efforts made on behalf of wild fish, waterfowl, wild turkeys, and other upland game species. This is partly because large mammals are more visible, and hearkening again back to Ernest Hemingway's line that "birds and fish lie weightless on the conscience," fishing and the hunting of feathered game have been somewhat less controversial than the hunting of large mammals. However, any discussion of North American wildlife conservation would be totally remiss in overlooking the amazing contribution of **Ducks Unlimited** (DU), founded in 1937 in the dark days of the Dust Bowl. One of several contributors to the length of our Great Depression, if not its origin, this climatic change of long-term drought greatly impacted waterfowl nesting conditions. It followed a long period of uncontrolled market gunning of waterfowl, which, together with greatly reduced production, had placed America's waterfowl in a precarious situation.

Ducks Unlimited was founded for the sole purpose of conserving waterfowl, accomplished primarily through conserving or restoring wetlands and nesting habitat. Although DU works hand in glove with state and federal agencies, its funding is private and its focus is international, with members and local chapters in Canada and Mexico as well as in the United States. In 2012 DU tallied five hundred forty-four thousand adult members and forty-eight thousand Greenwing youth members. Since its founding DU fund-raising banquets have become a fixture across North America, generating 3.68 billion dollars since 1937, 183.8 million dollars in 2011–2012 alone. An impressive eighty-three percent of all of DU's funds go straight to habitat improvement and the remainder to administration and fund-raising.

A primary focus has long been the critical prairie pothole nesting grounds in Canada, with 6,384,059 Canadian acres conserved by DU. In the United States the total acres conserved is 4,717,699 and in Mexico, 1,902,470. These are habitat projects considered complete; the total acreage that Ducks Unlimited has influenced, impacted, or improved on behalf of waterfowl is 104,844,741 acres (as of spring 2013). That's one hundred sixty-three thousand square miles, an area about the size of Kansas and Nebraska together.

The **Rocky Mountain Elk Foundation** (RMEF) is a relatively young organization, founded in 1984 primarily over concerns that critical winter habitats were being encroached at an alarming rate. It is probably important to note that the elk was not in trouble in 1984; it was in serious trouble in 1900 and rebuilt slowly through much of the twentieth century. But by 1984 many elk herds in both the United States and western Canada were starting to explode. Even so, winter range is a major factor for elk but also for human interests, including ranching, tourism development, suburban sprawl, and sometimes logging and mineral development.

The stated mission of RMEF is "to ensure the future of elk, other wildlife, their habitat and our hunting heritage." Thus, despite its specific name, RMEF isn't just for elk, also reaping dividends for other wildlife that shares elk habitat. By its mission statement it is also not a hunting organization but very much a pro-hunting organization, drawing its primary support from hunters. In support of this mission the RMEF is committed to (1) conserving, restoring, and enhancing natural habitats; (2) promoting the sound management of wild, free-ranging elk, which may be hunted or otherwise enjoyed; (3) fostering cooperation among federal, state, tribal, and private organizations and individuals in wildlife management and habitat improvement; and (4) educating members and the public about habitat conservation, the value of hunting, hunting ethics, and wildlife management.

Between its founding in 1984 and the end of 2012 RMEF conserved 6,287,980 acres of elk habitat. At 9,375 square miles, that's an area larger than Yellowstone, Grand Canyon, Glacier, Yosemite, Rocky Mountain, and Great Smoky Mountains National Parks combined. Direct conservation of critical habitat is obviously a major RMEF effort and focus, and this is actually accomplished in two ways. First and probably best—but most costly—is permanent land protection. Total for this category is 1,064,307 acres. Actual land acquisitions and conservation easements are the primary tools. The second habitat conservation strategy is stewardship projects, such as prescribed burns, forest thinning, and weed treatments, among other things. Total for this category is 5,223,673 acres. These projects tend to take less cash but more work. Either way, RMEF's primary funding *and* the majority of man-hours come from American hunters interested in elk.

While the elk has done well in the West, especially in recent years, the Eastern elk was exterminated early in the nineteenth century, and the Merriam's elk of the Southwest vanished in the early twentieth century. These are huge losses, gene pools now unknown and lost forever, but, unfortunately, extinction is final. However, the Rocky Mountain elk is very similar to these lost species and is capable of occupying the same habitat. The Merriam's elk were barely gone when elk from Yellowstone Park were restarted in their habitat, and of course have done very well for generations. In recent years elk have been reintroduced in the East, with significant breeding populations now reestablished in former ranges in numerous states, including Kentucky, New York, Pennsylvania, and Tennessee. RMEF has been involved in returning elk to six states and one national park, with Maryland now conducting a feasibility study.

Our various conservation organizations work in significantly different ways depending largely on their focus. As just mentioned, RMEF has focused heavily on land acquisition (or improvement) because so much critical winter range for elk is on private land. Similarly, DU's focus has been land because so much nesting habitat was at risk. The **Wild Sheep Foundation** (WSF), formerly known as the Foundation for North American Wild Sheep, was founded in 1977 when, despite a generation of effort by government agencies, many bighorn sheep (*Ovis canadensis*) levels were still remnant and in some states were reaching an all-time low.

Unlike Rocky Mountain elk, mule deer, and whitetail deer, the iconic bighorn lacked population numbers and hunting opportunity and hence license and tag fees to pay its own way. The WSF stepped into this gap created by the lack of state and provincial funding to properly manage and repatriate wild sheep to their native range. Their mission is simple and simply stated: "To put and keep sheep on the mountain." Since the majority of North American sheep habitat is on government land the WSF has not focused on land acquisition but rather has worked closely with state and federal wildlife managers, with typical projects including developing waterholes in desert mountains and reintroducing sheep into former—and sometimes altogether new—habitats.

The WSF's private funding from members and donors primarily has been raised at an annual fund-raising convention long known as "The Sheep Show." One important source of funding has been state-sponsored donations of governor's tags, now donated to the WSF and other organizations by many states (for many species), a creative fund-raising opportunity that has raised millions of dollars directly for conservation.

In 1980, with the sale of the first governor's sheep tag from Wyoming, the WSF and its partners began funding initiatives throughout North America to accomplish its purpose. Live-trapping and transplant projects were conducted across the West, initially bringing bighorns from Alberta and British Columbia south. Wildlife swaps occurred, with crazy stories of wild turkeys transported in private jets and traded for desert bighorn sheep. Relocation maps showing sheep transfers now look like an airline route map for a successful Western air carrier. The WSF, its chapters and affiliates, members, and agency partners *put sheep on the mountains* throughout their historical range. The results are a modern-day wildlife success story: Rocky Mountain, California, and desert bighorn sheep, which numbered around seventeen thousand in the 1960s, have been expanded fourfold to more than seventy thousand today.

Estimated Bighorn/Desert Bighorn Populations

	1960	2011	% Increase
Nevada	Remnant	10,000	
Colorado	3,000	7,500	250%
Wyoming	2,000	6,500	325%
Montana	1,700	5,100	300%
Utah	Remnant	5,000	
Texas	Remnant	1,100	
Washington	Remnant	1,700	
Arizona	3,500	5,500	57%
California	2,500	4,800	92%
Oregon	25	4,200	1,680%
Idaho	2,800	2,900	3%

Sources: Bueckner Monograph (1960) and Western Association of Fish & Wildlife Agencies (2011 data)

This amazing present-day conservation success story is a credit to the more than ten thousand WSF chapter and affiliate members worldwide and their dedication and contribution of thousands of man-hours of labor and dollars to bring wild sheep back from the brink. Realistically, the WSF has been so successful that in recent years it has become increasingly difficult to find new mountains to put sheep on, but the work of *keeping* sheep on the mountains is far from done. Knowledge gained from hundreds of thousands of dollars in disease research has proven unequivocally that the primary threat to keeping sheep on the mountain is ensuring that domestic sheep and goats are separated both spatially and temporally from bighorns. The WSF continues to lead efforts to protect wild sheep from bacteria from domestic livestock and works with the domestic sheep industry to seek collaborative solutions to this deadly problem.

During its most recent (2011–2012) fiscal year the WSF raised and put on the ground more than $3.6 million to mission programs directly benefiting wild sheep, other wildlife, and their habitats. This impressive amount equates to more than seven hundred dollars per member annually. For every membership dues dollar received, the WSF puts sixteen dollars on the ground in mission programs, an amazing and nearly unheard of sixteen-to-one multiplier. Combined with chapters and affiliates, since its founding in 1977, the WSF has raised and contributed more than eighty-five million dollars to putting and keeping wild sheep on the mountain.

We could go through the roll call of the many conservation organizations that draw their support from hunters, but the message should already be there: Hunters put their money where their mouths are. Safari Club International, for instance, is a larger, broader-focused organization with hundreds of chapters worldwide. As its motto states, it truly is "first for hunters," but it would be much more difficult and time consuming to encapsulate all of its efforts on behalf of both hunters and wildlife. But here's a good example of the generosity and dedication of today's hunters:

When the 2013 Safari Club convention was held in Reno it had just been announced that Zambia had specifically suspended lion and leopard hunting and was temporarily closing all hunting so that game management units could be reevaluated and reallocated. Under the table, the word on the street was that certain anti-hunting organizations had misrepresented U.S. Fish and Wildlife's position on lion hunting (specifically, stating that the United States had placed the lion on our own endangered species list, an action that has not occurred) and, as rumor has it, made some interesting promises to Zambia's Minister of Tourism and Arts, the Honorable Sylvia T. Masebo, who was in attendance at the SCI convention, asking for assistance with lion research and anti-poaching efforts. As further backdrop, the CITES Sixteenth Conference of the Parties was upcoming in Bangkok. One of the issues to be presented would be an effort by member states that have few or no remaining lions to force the uplisting of the African lion to endangered status. (This effort was defeated once again.)

On the last night of the convention SCI's executive director, Phil DeLone, got up on the stage and asked for pledges directly earmarked for lion management, protection, and enforcement and to further efforts to keep the lion as a huntable species. Within a few minutes the total exceeded 1.3 million dollars. These pledges were freely given, many by hunters who have not and probably never will hunt lion, and although the minister from Zambia was in the audience, there was absolutely no assurance (asked or given) that Zambia will ever again be open to lion hunting. It is to be hoped that Minister Masebo got the message and that our readers do as well: Many groups talk about conservation, but hunters put their money where their mouths are!

Chapter Fourteen

The Second Amendment

"A well-regulated Militia, being necessary to the security
of a free State, the right of the people to keep and bear
Arms, shall not be infringed."
—Amendment II of the Constitution of the
United States of America

T his is the Second Amendment to our Constitution as it was written and ratified, complete with eighteenth-century usage of commas and capitalization of key nouns. A version in more modern English might read "Because a well-regulated militia is necessary to national security, the right of the people to keep and bear arms may not be infringed." The exact meaning created by the commas and the relationship of the separate clauses (necessity of militia, the right to keep and bear arms) has been a matter of debate for many years. However, it's important to understand that our Second Amendment, as originally written, is part of America's binding and guiding document, our Constitution that remains our blueprint for government.

It is part of what we call our Bill of Rights, the first ten Amendments to our Constitution. These ten critical rights and freedoms were introduced to the First United States Congress by James Madison. Madison became our fourth president in 1809 but is also remembered as a key author to both our Constitution and the Bill of Rights. He actually introduced twelve amendments, adopted by the House of Representatives on August 21, 1789, and proposed by joint resolution of Congress as Constitutional Amendments on September 25, 1789.

Madison's first proposed amendment, Article I, on population numbers controlling the size of the House of Representatives was never ratified by the states. His second proposal, the original Article II, stated that "[n]o law varying the compensation for the services of the Senators and Representatives, shall take effect, until an election of Representatives shall have intervened." This proposed Amendment was not finally ratified for 203 years, becoming the Twenty-Seventh Amendment in 1992. The other ten original Amendments, including our Second Amendment, were ratified by three-fourths of the states and became Constitutional Amendments, part of the law of our land, on December 15, 1791.

We now know these first ten Amendments as the Bill of Rights because they include basic rights of our citizenry, including freedom of speech and religion, right to a speedy trial, protection from unlawful search and seizure, right to a jury trial, protection from excessive bail or fines and cruel and unusual punishments, and our right to keep and bear arms.

The background to our magnificent Bill of Rights is that, following our Revolution, there were major disagreements regarding the size and power of the federal government as opposed to the powers of the state governments. The Anti-Federalist faction was strong, and although the Constitution was ratified—with some difficulty—the controversy didn't go away. While most people today believe the American Civil War, fought eighty years later, was primarily over slavery, a majority of Americans who joined the Confederacy were not slaveholders but believed the conflict was over states' rights.

Many historians believe that a major issue in the Constitutional debates and one of the (few) major errors made by the framers of our Constitution was that it did not include a Bill of Rights. There were historical precedents, including the Virginia Declaration of Rights (1776) and the English Bill of Rights (1689). Such a bill was actually proposed during the Philadelphia Convention (1787), which created the Constitution, but it was proposed by Anti-Federalists opposed to the Constitution and was rejected. Two years later Madison's proposals intended to, and did, correct this omission. Although most of us best know our Bill of Rights as protecting individual liberties, the Ninth and Tenth Amendments act to limit the powers of federal government to matters specifically covered by the Constitution. The ten Amendments that comprise our Bill of Rights—including our Second Amendment—were ratified by the states with much less difficulty than the Constitution itself!

The American Revolutionary War began in 1775 and formally ended with the Treaty of Paris in 1783, a long, desultory, and often bitter struggle. Today we like to think that the war was won by frontiersmen with their Kentucky long rifles (actually, in those days they would properly have been *Pennsylvania* rifles), but this is not entirely accurate. The guerrilla warfare fought by armed Americans was a major thorn to the British but never decisive. In the early years of the war there were many incredibly courageous examples of poorly trained and equipped American militia standing up to British regulars. However, there were few instances of civilian militia *defeating* British regulars until General Washington was able to train a more or less proper European-style army. It's also a historical fact that French intervention finally turned the tide, pitting similarly armed and trained naval and ground forces against each other.

So, just a few years later, there's no question but that our founding fathers had the necessity for a well-regulated militia fresh in their minds. This was obviously to defend the newly minted United States against aggression. Not so obviously, remembering that an eight-year war against British oppression was fresh in their minds, both the militia and the "right of the people to keep and bear arms" formed a hedge against tyranny from within—against government that became too strong and was no longer "of the people, by the people, and for the people." The United States of America is among few nations on Earth that guarantees citizens the right to keep and bear arms in its founding and most revered body of law, but it does have precedence in English common law and the English Bill of Rights, which preceded it by a century.

In 1789 a large number of Americans hunted for subsistence, but target shooting (whether formal or informal) was relatively uncommon because powder and lead were too precious. Still, there is nothing in the Second Amendment or the rest of the Constitution that codifies hunting or other lawful uses of firearms as "rights." Since they are also not barred by the Constitution, we can consider them "privileges" subject to limitation by more local laws. However, the use of the term "defense" does codify that specific use of a firearm, although the exact interpretation has varied.

It is the duty of our United States Supreme Court not specifically to decide cases but to decide on the basis of constitutionality. There have been several important cases that have challenged, and in the main upheld, the Second Amendment's assertion that "the right of the people to keep and bear Arms, shall not be infringed." Perhaps the most ambiguous was the first, *United States vs. Cruikshank*, in 1875: "[T]he right to bear arms is not granted by the Constitution; neither is it in any manner dependent upon that instrument for its existence. The Second Amendment means that it (the right to keep and bear arms) shall not be infringed by Congress, and has no other effect than to restrict the powers of the National Government."

In *United States vs. Miller* (1939), the Supreme Court ruled that the Second Amendment protects arms that have a "reasonable relationship to the preservation or efficiency of a well-regulated militia." This is an interesting ruling, especially in light of the recent furor over "assault rifles." This will be discussed in greater detail in the next two chapters, but the type of firearm often referred to as an "AR" was mentioned briefly in Chapter 10 as the type of rifle Josh wanted to take on a wild hog hunt with his mom.

There is a huge confusion over definitions here. Some of it may be innocent based on ignorance; some of it is undoubtedly purposeful because assault rifles are evil. Here's the deal: An assault rifle is a military firearm with a very specific definition. It was developed in the latter days of World War II, and although the models differed, it was a parallel development by America, Germany, and Russia. The intent was to develop a weapon that had shorter range but lighter weight and greater firepower than did the "main battle rifle." As such, it was intended to offer an overwhelming volume of fire during an infantry assault, when range was short and long-range accuracy was not essential. The assault rifle had fully automatic capability, meaning that it continued to fire—like a machine gun—so long as the trigger remained depressed. A primary confusion is that what we today call an AR is based on the Armalite AR15 action, so in this context AR stands for Armalite Corporation, *not* assault rifle.

This action is indeed the basis for our military's M16 series of rifles, which do indeed have fully automatic capability, but the civilian ARs that are very popular today *do not* have this capability. They are semiautomatic, which means that they can fire only one time when the trigger is depressed. Semiautomatic sporting rifles, handguns, and shotguns have been available and popular since the early 1900s, and fully automatic firearms of any type have been illegal for general sale to the civilian market since 1934. The exception to this is a federal Class III license, which allows private ownership of fully automatic arms. This license is issued primarily to collectors and manufacturers, with rules varying considerably among the states. With the exception of the very few Class III license holders, it is safe to say that there are no assault rifles in legal civilian hands in the United States. There are, however, hundreds of thousands of semiautomatic sporting arms, some of which are based on civilianized look-alike versions of military actions. Many of them are ARs in semiautomatic form, an action so popular that today, in innumerable variations, it is manufactured by more than ninety companies.

If we held to the 1939 *U.S. vs. Miller* ruling, it would seem that, rather than being constantly vilified (and misclassified), this type of sporting rifle would be extremely desirable because, with operation and handling qualities similar to America's military rifle it clearly has a "reasonable relationship to the preservation or efficiency of a well-regulated militia."

Fortunately we have recent Supreme Court rulings that clarify the issue further and are much more in line with common understanding of the Second Amendment. In 2008, in *District of Columbia vs. Heller*, the Court ruling states that the Second Amendment "codified a pre-existing right," which refers back to English common law and the English Bill of Rights, upon which much of our own laws are based. Further, and more importantly, the Court ruling states that the Second Amendment "protects an individual's right to possess a firearm unconnected with service in a militia, and to use that arm for traditional lawful purposes, such as self-defense within the home." Although only self-defense is specifically mentioned, one might reasonably imply that other "traditional lawful uses" would include hunting, target shooting, and collecting. However, this ruling goes on to state that "the right is not unlimited. It is not a right to keep and carry any weapon whatsoever in any manner whatsoever and for whatever purpose." Most citizens and lawful gun owners would agree with this statement. Again, excepting a special and difficult-to-obtain license, fully automatic firearms have been illegal in civilian hands for a full generation, and states and local jurisdictions can and do enact rules regarding the lawful carry and use of firearms.

The most recent Second Amendment case to be ruled on by the Supreme Court is *McDonald vs. Chicago*, a complex case brought against the city of Chicago because of local legislation enacted that would, in effect create a ban on handgun ownership through draconian registration procedures. While not ruling on the specific issue, the Court ruled that the Second Amendment is incorporated by the due process clause of the Fourteenth Amendment, essentially limiting state and local government to the same extent that it limits the federal government. Interestingly, both the NRA and the Brady Campaign to Prevent Gun Violence were favorable toward the *McDonald vs. Chicago* decision, both agreeing that the Court's ruling protected specifically against bans on handguns for self-protection in the home.

This decision sparked a number of lawsuits against other local jurisdictions with severe restrictions on firearms (especially handguns), with numerous lawsuits still working their way through the judicial system. So, as the NRA stated after the *McDonald vs. Chicago* decision, the NRA "has a lot of work ahead." From the standpoint of both lawful gun owners and the anti-gun forces it is quite possible that the battle will never end, but after nearly 225 years America's Second Amendment still stands.

Although unfortunate, it is absolutely true that firearms have been and are being misused in our society—in direct contradiction of laws already in place. Even so and despite the current and justified wave of outrage against senseless acts of violence, according to recent surveys, a large majority of Americans still believe that the Second Amendment means what it says: "the right of the people to keep and bear Arms, shall not be infringed." A large number of these people believe that it is one of the cornerstones of American liberty. What do *you* believe?

✣ Chapter Fifteen ✣

Firearms, Hunting, and Conservation

In *District of Columbia vs. Heller* the United States Supreme Court validated "self-defense within the home" as a lawful use of a firearm. However, no ruling regarding the Second Amendment has ever specifically mentioned hunting in any context, although hunting would surely be considered one of several other "traditional lawful purposes" the same ruling referred to. This is not altogether inappropriate. If America has eighty million gun owners (even give or take ten or twenty million!) and a possible maximum of twenty million people who hunt (including occasional and infrequent hunters), then it's quite obvious that there are a lot more gun owners than hunters.

No single specific target-shooting discipline has as many followers as hunting, but there are dozens of formal target disciplines using all manner of firearms. There are millions more shooters who never enter formal competitions but enjoy a day at the range or simply plinking at tin cans against a hillside. And there are simply gun owners, ranging from avid collectors to the millions of people who keep a handgun or shotgun in the home "just in case."

The interesting anomaly is that not all gun owners are hunters and not all hunters own firearms. It's undoubtedly true that most do, but there are unknown thousands of dedicated bow hunters and archery target shooters who have no interest in firearms. But all gun owners, archers, and hunters share this: All contribute heavily to America's wildlife through the Wildlife Restoration Act excise tax on their equipment.

There have always been target shooters and gun owners who didn't hunt, but this legislation came about back in the 1930s. Times were different then. America's wildlife needed help! At that time America's population was much more rural, and during those Great Depression times subsistence hunting for small game was important. In 1935 the U.S. population was 127 million, about a third of our population today. It isn't known how many hunters there were at that time, probably not more than today and certainly not as many licensed hunters, but hunters were a much larger percentage of the U.S. population then. Target shooting was also extremely popular, but it's also likely that a much larger percentage of shooters were hunters. Our North American model of wildlife conservation was still developing, but by then it was in adolescence. Conservationists and legislators alike saw hunters and shooters—American gun owners in general—as the logical people to go to for extra help for wildlife.

By this time hunting licenses had long since been required in all states, and while a fair number of rural people were still flying under the radar and hunting illegally to put food on the table, there was a fast-growing consciousness that ethical hunting included buying the required licenses and adhering to seasons, bag limits, and the increasing full suite of hunting regulations. So wildlife management was being funded first by license sales, then by Pittman-Robertson funding, then by extras such as the duck stamp program, and finally by private conservation programs. Any citizen interested in wildlife is welcome to contribute, but the funding started with hunters.

The situation remains exactly the same today, with small exceptions. As bow hunting became an increasingly popular option the Pittman-Robertson excise tax was expanded to include archery tackle. Today gun owners and recreational shooters outnumber hunters, but these two groups together provide the lion's share of funding for North American wildlife management.

This has been stated previously but needs to be both restated and understood: There is no alternative funding in place! With hunters not only a shrinking minority compared to the U.S. population but apparently a shrinking minority within the larger community of gun owners, this raises interesting questions and challenges.

The anti-gun, and especially the anti-handgun and anti–assault rifle, forces have been strong for many years. The pro-firearms and pro–Second Amendment forces are also strong, but senseless acts of violence, such as the Sandy Hook massacre, have fueled a significant wave of anti-gun sentiment. The truth is we have plenty of laws already in place. In all too many of these tragedies one might point a finger at failure to enforce laws that we have and also a failure of our system of mental health care. The guns used, however, seem to be the easiest target.

At this writing it appears unlikely that significant federal gun-control legislation can be pushed through Congress, but in the wake of Sandy Hook a number of states have enacted restrictions on types of firearms that can be sold, magazine capacities, and so forth.

It is absolutely true that high-capacity firearms and, for that matter, semiautomatic firearms are not essential for hunting. We will come back to that. Perhaps surprisingly, however, it is also true that, according to a 2013 nationwide survey, public approval of *hunting* is at an eighteen-year high. The survey was conducted by Responsive Management, a public opinion research organization focusing on natural resources and outdoor recreation issues (not just hunting). They started tracking public opinion on hunting in 1995. Results for Americans who "strongly or moderately" approve of hunting were 1995, seventy-three percent; 2003, seventy-five percent; 2006, seventy-eight percent; 2011, seventy-four percent; and in the new 2013 survey, seventy-nine percent. According to that most recent 2013 survey fifty-two percent of Americans "strongly approve" of hunting, and only twelve percent "strongly or moderately" disapprove of hunting.

This is a very strong public mandate for the activity. While it is true that a small minority of serious bow hunters do not own firearms, most of America's hunters do own and use firearms. Thus it would seem that there is strong public support for hunting as a traditional and lawful use of firearms. Even though the great majority of Americans do not personally hunt and even the majority of gun owners do not, most support the activity. It could be inferred that even those who do not participate respect the individual choice to include hunting as a part of one's lifestyle. Just perhaps there is also growing awareness that hunters are the primary support for the wildlife that all Americans can enjoy in so many ways.

But let's get back to this business of good guns and bad guns. As stated earlier, fully automatic weapons—machine guns—have been illegal in civilian hands since 1934. Although some collectors love them—and there are federally administered licenses for collectors—chances are we can all agree that there is no sporting application, whether hunting or target shooting, for a fully automatic firearm. The same applies to explosive devices, which are covered under the same federal laws.

At this point it becomes much more difficult. Who, exactly, decides what differentiates a good gun from a bad gun? As mentioned more than once, what shooters like to term an AR (after Armalite's original AR15 action) or a modern sporting rifle is often mistakenly—or not so mistakenly—called an assault rifle by the anti-gun factions, some politicians, and members of the press. The modern sporting rifle is not an assault rifle. It is a semiautomatic sporting arm that happens to *look like* a military rifle. These firearms aren't just extremely popular today; they are the fastest-selling firearms in America. There are reasons for this. Culturally, with the Vietnam era a sad exception, Americans have long supported our military. The type of rifle used by our military has been popular with civilian shooters for more than a century. In these multimedia days it shouldn't be surprising that a lot of shooters desire a civilian look-alike of the rifles shown in the hands of our troops in print, film, and electronic media.

These modern sporting rifles are wonderfully accurate, fun to shoot, and also fun to accessorize with innumerable options in sights, stocks, handguards, and so much more. As stated previously, more than ninety firms are manufacturing semiautomatic sporting rifles on variations of the AR15 action, but there is also a huge industry making accessories of all types.

In appearance these are very nontraditional sporting arms. Not all gun owners or hunters like them, and quite a few want nothing to do with them. However, they can be effectively used for hunting, and many hunters choose them. There are two issues here that result in a major concern. First, it comes down to choice. Provided our choices are legal and cause no harm, we American hunters deserve the opportunity to choose the type of firearm we spend our hard-earned money on to take afield.

Second, remember that hunters as a group are no more than twenty-five percent of America's gun owners. Hunting as an activity has not been specifically validated by the U.S. Supreme Court—it is a privilege, not a right. However, hunting as a legitimate pursuit has been validated by public opinion. As the survey just referred to suggests, since 1995 the trend has been generally upward in approval of hunting. It could thus be inferred that the majority of the public believes that hunting is a legitimate and valid use of firearms and that, by extending that thought, firearms used by hunters are good guns. What about all the other firearms owned and used by possibly sixty million Americans who do not hunt? And who decides which are good guns and which are bad guns?

In the recent wave of anti-gun rhetoric, most experienced shooters (whether hunters or not) would have noticed that most people making their bold anti-gun statements don't know much about firearms (witness the assault rifle misnomer) and that all too many who should know don't know much about the laws currently in place. There is another disturbing trend. Various politicians and pundits, from President Obama on down, specifically stated something like this: "We don't want to take away the hunters' guns."

As stated, many hunters prefer more traditional firearms than the modern sporting rifles. It is also true that there are many types of firearms suited and legal for hunting, including types of handguns in most states. So the disappearance of the modern sporting rifle as an option for hunting would not close hunting, and might not significantly impact hunter numbers. But would the lack of that choice cure the problems of American society? This business of "we don't want the hunters' guns" is pure validation of the legitimacy of hunting in America. It is also frightening. Do the anti-gun forces see a division between hunters and all other gun owners? Would they like to drive a wedge between the two groups and then divide and conquer?

From the standpoint of both groups this would be a disaster. A united group of eighty million Americans, hunters and gun owners together, represents an almost unassailable block. Hunters are not a small group, but they represent a much smaller minority. And gun owners in general benefit from public approval of hunting as a legitimate use of firearms.

It could also be a disaster for American wildlife. While hunters, through license sales, fund the majority of the costs for America's wildlife management, the contribution of all other gun owners through the Pittman-Robertson excise tax cannot be ignored. One effect of the anti-gun rhetoric and threats of gun-control legislation in 2012–2013 has been to drive sales of firearms and ammunition to an all-time high. Some of it is panic buying, some of it is hoarding, and in many cases considered and rational decisions are being made that it's time to own a firearm and learn how to use it. Ah, but purely from a conservation standpoint, the influx of bonus funds from the excise tax is going to do wonders for American wildlife!

The recent increase in hunting license sales has, literally, saved the wildlife departments of numerous states from bankruptcy. The influx of Pittman-Robertson money, often distributed as matching funds, will allow many state agencies to undertake projects they have long dreamed of. Yes, sports men and women will benefit. But America's wildlife is the real beneficiary along with all Americans who enjoy wildlife in any way.

And the converse, with gun owners outnumbering hunters three to one, the contribution of America's firearms industry and non-hunting gun owners to American wildlife cannot be underestimated. That three-to-one disparity was probably not envisioned as our North American model developed, but that's where we are. There is no alternative funding, and any serious degradation in the huge community of American gun owners will have a negative impact on American wildlife.

✢ Chapter Sixteen ✢

Guns and American Society

According to the most recent census the U.S. population was about three hundred five million and growing. No one knows exactly how many firearms there are in the United States. One estimate, derived from a survey commissioned by the U.S. Congress, suggests that the number could be as high as three hundred million. That's a lot of guns, almost enough for every man, woman, and child in the country to own one! Clearly not every American owns one, even though there are almost enough to go around. Children may have adult-owned firearms they are allowed to use but cannot legally own themselves. Neither can convicted felons, persons with any history of domestic violence, nor people judged mentally defective or unstable. These are laws long in place.

We also know that many millions of perfectly normal law-abiding Americans do not own firearms. Once again, according to the National Rifle Association, there are an estimated eighty million lawful gun owners in the United States. If that figure is reasonably accurate, then gun owners as a group would need to own an average of less than four firearms each to reach that amazing figure of three hundred million. This is not far-fetched at all. Millions of lawful gun owners have a single handgun or shotgun for defense of the home. Some hunters may have but a single shotgun or rifle, but very large numbers of hunters and gun owners possess multiple firearms for different purposes: a shotgun for bird hunting, a center-fire rifle for deer hunting, a .22 for small game and low-cost target practice, and perhaps a handgun for personal defense.

In other countries citizens are often limited by law as to the number of firearms they are allowed to own. Thanks to the Second Amendment protection Americans enjoy, this is not the case in the United States. There are avid shooters and hunters who own, enjoy, and use dozens of different firearms, and there are collectors who own firearms into the hundreds. It isn't difficult to envision a very large total number for America's estimated eighty million gun owners.

Canadian citizens lack the Second Amendment protection of their cousins to the south. Historically handgun ownership has been more restricted in Canada, but Canadians have enjoyed much the same access to long firearms—shotguns and rifles—as do U.S. citizens. A few years ago Canada attempted total registration and licensing of all firearms, with limits on ownership. It turned into a bureaucratic nightmare that cost billions of dollars and was more or less abandoned. This is a lesson for the United States. We do not have firearms registration per se, and going in that direction would be exceedingly difficult even if the Second Amendment were overturned. However, in this computerized age we do have very good records of (recent) legal purchases of all firearms through dealers. Provided thefts are reported and proper information given, we also have a very good national registry of stolen firearms.

Although this diminishes over time, millions of unrecorded firearms remain in the United States, passed down through the generations and transferred in private sales. There is also an illegal black market, no blacker and no less illegal than trade in heroin and crystal meth. It is inevitable that some firearms will find their way into the hands of criminals, who will obtain them by hook or by crook. This is part of the cost of a free society, the law-abiding citizens of which have had the right to own firearms since America became a nation. Criminals have never had this right, but they steal it. Any violent crime is a tragedy, and any crime involving a firearm is both a tragedy and an insult to the millions and millions of law-abiding, safety-conscious American hunters and shooters.

That said, criminals *will* obtain firearms. Occasionally they will use them to commit crimes. One of the National Rifle Association's old slogans was "[w]hen guns are outlawed only outlaws will have guns." This remains true.

It doesn't matter whether law-abiding citizens are able to obtain firearms or not. Serious criminals will have them, and law-abiding people will not be able to exercise their currently lawful option to possess a firearm for personal defense in the home.

All violent crime is terrible. The really awful incidents, such as Columbine and Sandy Hook, are completely beyond understanding. Knee-jerk reactions, such as blaming the guns, are understandable, but with so many millions of firearms in the United States it would be very difficult to get that genie back in the bottle. Firearms are not unrestricted in the United States. Many states and municipalities make it much more difficult to purchase a handgun than a rifle or shotgun. Background checks are now nearly universal, and waiting periods between purchase and pickup are becoming much more common. Using a firearm in a crime generally carries a much more severe penalty than does committing a crime without one. We do need to rigidly enforce the laws we have, not necessarily create more laws that will almost exclusively restrict law-abiding citizens.

The reality is that only a very small fraction of the hundreds of millions of American firearms are ever used in any criminal act whether petty or horrific. The anti-gun factions would have us believe that gun crime is on the rise, and indeed, thanks to the sensationalist press, it would seem that this must be true. In fact, it is not. According to the Pew Research Center, firearms-related deaths peaked in 1993 and since then have dropped a whopping forty-nine percent.

It can be agreed that any unnecessary death is a terrible thing. But death is the ultimate end of life, and in a nation of more than three hundred million people deaths will occur. Using available figures, the leading cause of death in America is heart disease, which claimed nearly six hundred thousand lives in 2010. In the same year cancer was second at five hundred seventy-five thousand. In the same year there were 11,078 firearms-related deaths, which includes accidental as well as criminal. This is quite far down the list of causes of death in America, quite far below the deaths from medical malpractice. Even so, it's a large number. However, the number alone does not offer a complete picture: Something like a third of all firearms-related deaths are suicides. This is an avoidable loss, but it suggests at least as much a failure of our mental health care as the simple availability of a firearm.

The majority of deaths caused by firearms are from handguns. And yet the current wave of anti-gun rhetoric is directed against semiautomatic rifles, the so-called (but incorrectly identified) assault rifles. In 2010 total deaths attributed to *rifles* was 358, which includes semiautomatic sporting rifles.

Handguns clearly cause much more mayhem, and, in almost all American jurisdictions, handguns have much more stringent controls and regulations than do long guns, both to buy and to use. We can go back once more to the Supreme Court ruling that validated use of a firearm "for traditional lawful purposes, such as self-defense within the home." The same ruling went on to state: "[T]he right is not unlimited. It is not a right to keep and carry any weapon whatsoever in any manner whatsoever and for whatever purpose." Fair enough. It's one thing to keep a firearm in the home for personal defense and defense of one's family; it's another to carry a firearm at work and at play, as a part of life. We have laws to cover that. They vary considerably from place to place, but it is generally legal to transport a cased and unloaded firearm, and it is generally illegal to carry a concealed firearm without a special permit. Even transporting a firearm in a vehicle is subject to local rules (and if you're going from state to state, such as on a hunting trip or to a shooting event, it's wise to know those rules!).

One might reasonably question *why* there has been such a drop in deaths from gunshot wounds in the past twenty years. It is clearly not because there are fewer guns on the streets. Hunter numbers are up, recreational shooting is up, and especially in the past few years firearms sales are at an all-time high. Without question stiffer penalties for crimes involving firearms are a factor. However, there may be another factor, and that's the concealed carry revolution. Not terribly long ago it was extremely difficult in many jurisdictions to obtain a permit to carry a concealed weapon. Our world is not always as safe as we wish it were. Many neighborhoods are plagued by gang wars and drug-related violence, and the entire length of our southern border is fraught with danger. Police men and women aren't always as close at hand as we wish, so part of the reason for the rise in firearms sales and gun ownership, especially among women, is the desire to use the legal option we have to keep a firearm to defend our homes.

Dozens of states have carried this a step further, offering a concealed carry permit that, with approved formal training and appropriate background checks, is much more available than ever before. This is not universal. These permits are reciprocal in some states and not in others, and there are plenty of no firearms allowed areas. Airports, courtrooms, and other public buildings are obvious, but in most jurisdictions all a business owner needs to do is post a no firearms allowed sign or a firearm within a crossed red circle—like a no smoking sign—and the carry permit is not valid on those premises and thus carrying is illegal.

Here's the interesting thing: In every jurisdiction where carry laws have been liberalized violent crime has gone down. Period, end of story. Criminals are basically lazy cowards, on the lookout for a soft target, the softer the better. Not knowing exactly who is armed but knowing a significant percentage of the population is increases the risk and reduces motive and opportunity.

This book does not suggest that every American household should be armed. However, choosing to own a firearm "for any traditional and lawful purpose" is a legal option for American adults in good standing. The evidence is clear that this option should remain, but it carries responsibility as well as a sense of security. People who haven't grown up around firearms and have little or no familiarity should give somber reflection before willy-nilly running out and purchasing a gun.

Part of the responsibility is learning how to use it safely, correctly, and legally. To use a firearm for self-defense you must *have* a firearm, and before you have one you should know under what circumstances you might legally use it in your area. Generally speaking, it is legal to use a firearm in self-defense if you are legitimately in fear of your life. But beyond a genuine and provable life-threatening situation, the rules vary, and every gun owner needs to know them. Again, the Internet is an invaluable tool, and the NRA and many other organizations offer low- or no-cost seminars. This training is invariably part of concealed carry training, so this training is recommended whether one intends to actually (ever) carry a firearm or even complete the licensing procedures.

Learning safe handling is mandatory, and learning to shoot accurately simply makes sense. There are plenty of options for this, covered in previous chapters, but it's not only silly to own a firearm without making the commitment to learn how to use it safely and properly; it's downright dangerous.

The other required commitment is not just to use the firearm safely but to *keep it safely*. Every household is different, but it should be obvious that firearms cannot be left lying around in homes with small children. Family training is also required and also safekeeping measures, from full-up gun safes to a securely locked drawer. Although they are rare, every year there are accidents from children playing with guns. There is truly no excuse for this, but a person considering owning a firearm for the first time should think about his or her entire household, how it's managed and how that firearm will be safeguarded.

Millions of Americans have considered these things and joined the ranks of American gun owners. Some have become avid shooters; others have received a bit of training and filed it away just in case. Guns have been a part of American society since the Pilgrims landed. Their lawful use remains an integral part of American society today, and the option remains available to maintain a firearm for personal defense. This option is not for everyone, but it is being embraced by thousands and thousands of new gun owners, and whether any particular American chooses to embrace it, it is part of our heritage and birthright.

✥ Chapter Seventeen ✥

A Look Ahead

There is no reason for gloom and doom, but there is also no point in whistling one's way through a graveyard. In this year of 2013 there is much to be positive about regarding wildlife and hunting, especially here in North America. However, with our own ever-more-urbanized society and the world's burgeoning human population, there is much to be concerned about.

In North America, at this snapshot in time, we seem to have turned a corner. U.S. Fish and Wildlife's 2011 National Survey of Fishing, Hunting, and Wildlife-Associated Recreation shows a very significant nine percent increase in hunter numbers over the 2006 survey. This is the first verified increase in hunter participation in many years, and it suggests that sports men and women have taken heed of our own rhetoric and gotten serious about recruiting new hunters. A few years ago the Florida wildlife department held a summit conference, and the department was quite frank about the problem in Florida: Numbers were falling, and if they couldn't turn it around they would go broke. Thanks to aggressive youth programs, mentoring programs, hunter education, grassroots efforts, and a fine public relations effort the department turned it around, as have many U.S. state agencies in the past few years. Yet another recent survey shows the highest public approval for hunting since this subject was tracked.

In the United States there is another huge bonus headed for American wildlife. We have discussed the Wildlife Recovery Act, aka Pittman-Robertson, the excise tax on firearms, ammunition, and archery equipment parceled out to the states. This is the law of unintended consequences in its finest hour. There is no need to discuss politics in any way here; regardless of which side of the aisle you sit on or how you might have voted, it must be acknowledged that President Barack Obama is the most effective gun salesman who ever lived. Since his election in 2008 firearms and ammunition sales have been brisk, and states have been reaping the benefits. Since his second election, followed by the Sandy Hook tragedy and concerns over proposed legislation, firearms and ammunition sales have been unprecedented. It really doesn't matter what you think about that phenomenon. It is simple fact, and the extension of that fact is that, as a result, state wildlife agencies are going to be better funded, which, from a pure wildlife management standpoint, is a very good thing.

There are concerns relative to this issue, though. When the Pittman-Robertson legislation came into being it was probably believed that hunting was a primary reason for firearms ownership in the United States. Whether true or not, in a much less urban pre–World War II America, finding a place to shoot was not a problem. Things have changed. Considering the hunters who, by age, are not required to buy licenses and adding in people who may not participate (buy licenses) every year or even every other year but still consider themselves hunters, we might be able to stretch the point and come up with twenty million hunters in the United States. This is a very large number, by far the largest hunting society and culture on the face of the Earth. However, it's not a big number compared to total gun owners, who, as we've seen, the National Rifle Association estimates may be eighty million.

The simplest arithmetic suggests that hunting is no longer the dominant reason for Americans owning firearms. There are, of course, lots of other good reasons, from collecting to target shooting (formal and informal) to personal defense, but here's the point: The millions of gun owners who do not hunt pay the same excise tax on their equipment as those who do, but they aren't necessarily getting their money's worth. There are no audible complaints about this, but most Americans believe strongly in the concept of fair play. Especially with the bounty forthcoming from current panic buying of firearms and hoarding of ammunition, one might theorize that our state wildlife agencies increasingly owe it to American gun owners to put some of that money back into public-range facilities. Many states recognize this situation and are doing exactly that, but these programs need to be expanded.

Another concern *is* about politics. As stated earlier, it appears that anti-gun politicians would like to drive a wedge between hunters and shooters and exploit that wedge to the detriment of both. Defining good guns and bad guns is a slippery slope, and it seems obvious that this tactic is designed to separate the hunters and the gun owners. If you are in neither camp this may not be as difficult as it sounds. Some bow hunters don't own firearms, and many hunters who own only, say, sporting shotguns and perhaps a bolt-action rifle simply don't understand the fuss. The fuss is this: While some state constitutions do validate hunting as a right, the U.S. Constitution does not. The Second Amendment guarantees the right to keep and bear arms, and fully automatic firearms have been illegal in civilian hands since 1934. It is dangerous to erode the Second Amendment, and no shooters want politicians telling them which firearms are suited for hunting, the various shooting sports, and other lawful applications. It is really important for hunters and gun owners to maintain a united front on this or else America will be far down that slippery slope before we realize the first step was taken.

We'll come back to a snapshot of our North American model of wildlife conservation, but let's leave our own continent for now and take a whirlwind tour around the globe. In **Europe** wildlife management is generally quite mature. Their system isn't the same as ours, but it obviously works. It places a huge burden upon a relatively small number of hunters, but they seem to shoulder it gladly, with numbers holding fairly steady in most countries. Remembering that plaque on a lonely road in Scotland brings to mind that most European countries similarly eradicated their wolves and other major predators and so have been able to manage their wildlife in an environment artificially predator free. This is changing. Wolves are coming back, but now they are sacred cows! In Sweden and Finland the moose is an important crop, both culturally and economically, but wolves (protected, of course) are increasing rapidly and are starting to have an effect. There may be some hard lessons before tough decisions can be taken.

Asia is such a huge land mass that generalizations are dangerous. Turkey and Russia, for instance, generally follow the European model, but in much of Asia—Indonesia, Malaysia, and India—it's almost too late for wildlife to have a chance. But, to make one of those dangerous generalizations, in Asia, wildlife is either *gone* or continues to be utilized. The utilization is either unregulated (illegal) subsistence hunting, which will continue until the resource is exhausted, or regulated sport hunting, which places value on the resource. The value placed is often extreme, which sharply limits the market but provides incentive for conservation. This is not much different from the European model, except that the great majority of the hunters (and the funds) are foreign.

This concept has long-term issues, as was the case in China when a growing middle class found it unacceptable that hunting permits were offered only to foreigners. Although illegal subsistence hunting (poaching) continues in China's back country, its once-lucrative and well-organized sport-hunting program has now been closed for a decade while the country wrestles with this problem. Other emerging Asian countries may eventually have similar issues, but in the short-term wildlife is secure and frequently gaining ground in Asia's hunting countries and continuing to dwindle in countries that place no value on their wildlife.

The biggest problem in **Africa** is habitat loss, a creeping scourge caused by human overpopulation. There appears to be no long-term solution, so, regrettably, it seems almost inevitable that a time will come when ever-shrinking and increasingly encroached parks and reserves are the only enclaves for African wildlife. Some countries are already there, and this is not a process that easily can be reversed. Fortunately Africa is a very big continent and still has a lot of wild country holding a lot of wildlife. As discussed elsewhere in this volume, Africa's hunting countries, by placing value on wildlife, are doing far and away the best job of balancing human need (and greed) for land against room for wildlife. The human tide can be held back for some years to come, but, ultimately, because of Africa's unique problems the privatization of wildlife, which is anathema to our North American model, is probably the best hope in the long term. The best current examples are South Africa and Namibia, together with the private conservancies in Zimbabwe, but private lands in Botswana and Zambia are also providing an excellent example by conserving wildlife because of its value.

The situation in what we hunters call the **South Pacific**, a nonsensical collection of the continent of Australia and the island nations of New Caledonia, New Guinea, and New Zealand, is a bit different from the rest of the world in that the major wildlife populations are nonnative, introduced species. This often makes them dangerous to native flora, if not fauna, so it's a constant dilemma as to whether their populations should be managed or tolerated at all. Both Australia and New Zealand have conducted extensive and expensive eradication campaigns against various species—against the outrage of sports men and women and, in some cases, anti-hunters, in a unique partnership—but in both countries the genie was too far out of the bottle to be affordably rebottled. Both countries seem to have achieved a compromise with their nonnatives, with some areas kept clean and other areas either managed by and for sport hunters or left alone.

Perhaps some of global wildlife's greatest challenges—and opportunities—lie in **South America**. Argentina is a notable exception, but in general South America is at least a generation behind its northern neighbors in wildlife management, perhaps primarily because this has not been a focus. The majority of native large mammals are considered endangered. In some cases this is a correct classification; in others it is based on lack of scientific knowledge, which requires both human will and funding to obtain. Few Latin American countries have hunting laws in effect, which means that subsistence and other forms of hunting continue in the absence of law rather than under its guidance.

The good news is that it is not too late. Key native species, such as marsh deer, pampas deer, jaguar, spectacled bear, and many others, have indeed vanished from vast tracts of former range, but South America is a big place. As far as is known no major species have become extinct, and pockets remain, with good populations of most. A number of South American countries, including Bolivia, Brazil, Paraguay, Peru, and Venezuela are working toward better protection of their wildlife, including establishment of hunting laws. There is much work to be done, but there is both interest and hope.

Finally, let's return home to **North America**. Our North American model of wildlife conservation has been wildly successful, literally turning around what was indeed a grim situation less than a century ago. It is not a model with universal applicability, but it does offer some lessons that have worldwide value. It must also be understood that, in Canada and the United States, we have enjoyed several human generations of domestic tranquility and relative prosperity. These have allowed greater focus on conserving our natural resources—including wildlife—than has been possible in many other countries. Mexico, for instance, is making great strides today but still has much work to do. So we have the luxury of science-based wildlife management under a system of laws, and we have used hunters and hunting as the primary base to fund these efforts.

It is thus probably most appropriate to conclude this discussion with a review of that North American model, with an eye toward the challenges that we face currently and in years to come. Fortunately we don't have to rely altogether on individual and limited observations or a faulty crystal ball. In early 2013 The Wildlife Society and the Boone and Crockett Club jointly published *The North American Model of Wildlife Conservation Technical Review 12-04, December 2012*. Together they bring a highly credible and experienced perspective to the challenges that lie ahead.

Wildlife resources are a public trust. This is the lynchpin of our wildlife policy and management. It remains strong, but there are challenges. A long-standing issue has been the disposition and status of wild animals found on privately owned land, in other words, the conflict between the rights of property owners and the concept of wildlife as a public trust. This has traditionally been a compromise in that the harvesting and management of wildlife on private land is subject to the same laws applicable on public lands, with the notable exception that trespass rights are retained by the landowner. In today's world this is complicated by the proliferation of game-proof fences. Obviously this currently applies much more in some areas than in others, but the question remains: At what point do wild animals cease being wild and become instead livestock? Some jurisdictions make exceptions for game farms and such; others do not, but the commercialization of wildlife on private land, which can be a very good business for the landowner, poses a threat to the public trust doctrine.

The animal rights movement itself is a threat since it rejects ownership of animals, including by the public. Neither the animal rightists nor the North American model has an alternative solution.

Markets for game are eliminated. This principle stems from the disastrous and unregulated market hunting of the nineteenth century and, in the case of waterfowl, well into the twentieth. In general, market hunting has been eliminated, but this is not entirely consistent. Trapping of furbearers is a market, explained in that it is a licensed and regulated harvest that assists in the management of predator populations but still inconsistent with this tenet of the model. There are also markets for fish and certain reptiles, including turtles and alligators. But, returning to the game farms mentioned above, there is active trading in whitetail deer, elk, nonnative species, and a variety of game birds.

Experts on the North American model argue that there can be exceptions if a conservation purpose is served. As discussed previously, value to hunters has fostered the propagation in the United States of numerous species now scarce in their native lands, so this is an exception with a positive benefit. One might argue further that, as hunting opportunity becomes more elusive, the opportunity, for example, to harvest pen-reared pheasants serves as a valuable tool for both recruiting and training. But the growing market (and increasing prices) for hunting leases starts to lean toward the European model and runs the risk of making hunting unaffordable to many Americans.

Allocation of wildlife is by law. It is clearly understood that it is the mandate of the states to set seasons, bag limits, and establish licensing procedures. These vary dramatically based on a state's management goals and challenges, and enforcement also varies. According to *Technical Review 12-04*, however, a major challenge to this tenet is that local ordinances often supersede state authority, restricting or eliminating hunter access. Changing land use may adversely impact wildlife, reducing wildlife available to be allocated. As America continues to become more urbanized and suburban sprawl continues, hunting opportunity will become an ever-increasing issue in maintaining America's hunting culture. This is not a small concern because the North American model is built around a large hunting public.

Wildlife can be killed only for a legitimate purpose. Here there may be distinctions between legal and legitimate, the former meaning within the game laws of the jurisdiction where the hunt is conducted and the latter implying the application of a moral compass. Key to the North American model is that hunters are sports men and women, pursuing their sport ethically, with no profit motive and for no commercial purpose, and that no game killed is wasted. The American term "varmint" is a corruption of the English word "vermin" and is applied to a large class of wildlife generally considered nonedible: rodents, small predators, and crows. Such taking of wildlife is legally sanctioned in many jurisdictions, and one could argue that controlling the numbers of animals detrimental to agricultural concerns or other animal populations serves a legitimate purpose. But does this violate the principle that game is not wasted? This is a gray area, but hunters who take only the horns or antlers without recovering the meat have crossed from gray into black.

Fortunately most states have wanton waste game laws, which make it mandatory to recover edible meat, an ethic that shouldn't require laws to enforce. But these days more and more American hunters are increasingly trophy conscious, all too many to the point of obsession. Many hunters are admitted trophy hunters in that, in many situations, they consciously seek the oldest and largest animal they can find. But they don't waste game meat, and hopefully they prize the quality of the hunt more than the quality of the animal. In most well-developed animal populations good management requires the taking of more than just the older, nonbreeding males, and certainly, in accordance with the North American model, there is not a huge trophy for every hunter.

Hunters' record books serve a marvelous purpose in showing us the potential our game has for full development and as a research tool in showing where the "big ones" come from, but an increasing fixation on trophy size is a challenge to this tenet and thus to our North American model. Ultimately it should be about the hunt and about managing and properly utilizing our wildlife.

Wildlife is considered an international resource. The United States has a long history of collaboration with Canada: Our Migratory Bird Treaty goes back to 1916 and was actually negotiated with Great Britain on behalf of Canada. Efforts with Mexico are more recent but are ongoing and have included introduction of South Dakota bison into Coahuila. The most significant wildlife-related international treaty is CITES, which the United States ratified in 1975.

As we have tried to export democracy, so have we tried to export our North American model of conservation, with U.S. Fish and Wildlife biologists active in many areas around the globe. There have been some successes, but culture, traditions, and even firearms restrictions in many countries have suggested that our model is not suited for every nation. The greatest current challenge on our own continent is the drug and immigration skirmishes along the U.S.–Mexican border, which clearly impact wildlife and the free movement of border species. However, American hunters are the world's largest hunting culture and thus by far the world's largest group of traveling international hunters. U.S. Fish and Wildlife often holds U.S. hunters to higher standards than does CITES regarding issuance of permits and importation of trophies. This fact, plus an international view that the U.S. is increasingly allowing politics rather than science to dictate wildlife policy (as illustrated by the recent U.S. initiative to uplist the polar bear), has eroded U.S. credibility with CITES. By extension, from a world view this undermines the credibility of the North American model.

Science is the proper tool to discharge wildlife policy. The United States and Canada have led the world in advancing professional, science-based wildlife management, and the benefits of our system and model can be seen throughout the continent. However, once again the greatest challenge appears to be the often ugly specter of politics. State agency directors and state game boards and commissions are often political appointees, with high turnover rates based on election results. On an increasing basis, some studies and positions appear to be flavored by politics rather than by pure science, the polar bear initiative again remaining a fine example.

Certain decisions have occasionally caused the U.S. Fish and Wildlife to be demonized by pro-hunting groups. Sometimes this appears justified, but there is a practical political reality: Sound wildlife decisions that appear pro-hunting are likely to bring lawsuits from anti-hunting groups (the reverse also applies). The extension of this reality is that budget and personnel constraints and legal costs—even at the federal level—may dictate no action when the course of the proper tool, science, should be clear. Politics thus appears to be a current and increasing challenge to this tenet of our North American model.

Democracy of hunting is standard. The citizenry of few other nations on Earth have the opportunity to hunt as that enjoyed in the United States and Canada, a concept that is key to our demonstrably successful system of wildlife management. It is clear that the majority of people in both countries choose not to participate, but all good citizens have the legal opportunity. Of key importance, our professional wildlife managers rely almost exclusively on the support of the millions who do. Even so, it must be understood that hunters are a minority group. Genuine anti-hunters are perhaps an even smaller minority, but they are dedicated, driven, often organized, and politically adept.

Numerous backdoor anti-hunting measures have been pushed through via ballot initiatives—California's transfer of the cougar from a game animal to a nongame species, essentially a sacred cow that the state game department is no longer allowed to manage—remains an early and classic example. Other ballot initiatives have followed in other states. Some have been defeated, and others have passed. But the concept clearly violates the principle that science is the proper tool. And since this tactic has worked, it has become a weapon of choice, attacking certain hunting seasons and methods of take (such as hound hunting) that are poorly understood by the non-hunting majority. Many battles lie ahead.

Earlier in this chapter concern was voiced that restrictive firearms legislation could impact hunting and thus our system of wildlife management. Lest this be considered alarmism, here is a direct quote from *Technical Review 12-04*, under "Current Status, Threats, and Challenges" to the tenet that democracy of hunting is standard: "[A]ccess to firearms and gun control restrictions directly impact the public's ability to hunt. . . . Clearly most North Americans do not hunt in the traditional sense of the word. We believe that our current pluralistic democracy is necessary for the Model's survival. Without secure gun rights, the average person's ability to hunt would likely be compromised, along with indispensable sources of funding for implementation of the Model."

Our system is not perfect, but the North American model of wildlife conservation has brought this continent's wildlife from rags to riches in a single century. It is based on Theodore Roosevelt's belief that "access for all to have the opportunity to hunt would result in many societal benefits." It is not expected that all citizens will choose to explore this opportunity, but it is expected that those who choose not to participate respect the choice of those who do.

Our incredibly successful model is further based on the concept that those who participate will shoulder the major financial burden of conserving and managing our wildlife for the benefit of all. Those who seek to end hunting in North America are indeed seeking the downfall of our wildlife because, as the Arizona game department states so simply, "*There is no alternative funding.*"